CLASH
OF
CROWNS

To Anne

Thank you for everything

S. D. G.

CLASH
OF
CROWNS
THE BATTLE OF BYLAND

Robert the Bruce's Forgotten Victory

HARRY PEARSON

Pen & Sword
MILITARY

AN IMPRINT OF PEN & SWORD BOOKS LTD.
YORKSHIRE - PHILADELPHIA

First published in Great Britain in 2024 by
PEN AND SWORD MILITARY
An imprint of
Pen & Sword Books Limited
Yorkshire – Philadelphia

ISBN 978 1 39903 591 0

A CIP catalogue record for this book is available from the British Library.

Typeset in Times New Roman 11.5/14 by
SJmagic DESIGN SERVICES, India.
Printed and bound in the UK by CPI Group (UK) Ltd.

Pen & Sword Books Limited incorporates the imprints of Atlas, Archaeology,
Aviation, Discovery, Family History, Fiction, History, Maritime, Military,
Military Classics, Politics, Select, Transport, True Crime, Air World, Frontline
Publishing, Leo Cooper, Remember When, Seaforth Publishing, The Praetorian
Press, Wharncliffe Local History, Wharncliffe Transport, Wharncliffe True Crime
and White Owl.

For a complete list of Pen & Sword titles please contact
PEN & SWORD BOOKS LIMITED
George House, Units 12 & 13, Beevor Street, Off Pontefract Road,
Barnsley, South Yorkshire, S71 1HN, England
E-mail: enquiries@pen-and-sword.co.uk
Website: www.pen-and-sword.co.uk

or

PEN AND SWORD BOOKS
1950 Lawrence Rd, Havertown, PA 19083, USA
E-mail: uspen-and-sword@casematepublishers.com
Website: www.penandswordbooks.com

Contents

Statue of King Robert the Bruce at the entrance to Edinburgh Castle. (Author)

A selection of Reviews of
'Clash of Crowns'

"To mark the 700th anniversary of the battle of Byland, Harry Pearson has produced an excellent account of the engagement set in its context. His clear and unfussy narrative provides a tour of the earlier stages of the Anglo-Scottish conflict begun in the reign of Edward I through to the detail of the battle itself and the aftermath concluding with the Treaty of Edinburgh / Northampton in 1328 which ended the first phase of the Wars of Scottish Independence and which gave the Scots all that they had been fighting for.

This book is readily accessible to the non-specialist reader while underpinned with notes and a bibliography for those who may wish to delve into the detail of the primary and secondary sources.

The precise location of the battle has been the subject of some debate over the years and Harry Pearson has put forward his views based on detailed research and an intimate knowledge of the landscape. By way of appendices there is a helpful section on the arms and armour of the period and a brief summary of the limited archaeological investigations that have taken place to date. The book concludes with some suggested battlefield walks for those who wish to visit the site.

Harry Pearson has illustrated his text throughout with photographs and maps that bring the landscape and the story to life.

Overall this is a highly readable and clear account of a battle that deserves to be better known and remembered."
Geoffrey Carter, the Battlefields Trust.

"Harry Pearson has achieved an extraordinary feat with his book Clash of Crowns. He has brought the Battle of Byland to life and carried out extensive historical research on a previously forgotten Yorkshire conflict. The book is captivating, enthralling and engaging in telling the story of a highly significant battle between the English and the Scots in 1322. His work has had a lasting impact in enabling a permanent and beautiful monument at the top of Sutton Bank. I am grateful that Harry has worked with local schools, including my own and the community to bring this important story to life."

Pete Jackson, Head of History, Ryedale School, North Yorkshire.

"Harry Pearson has written an absolutely amazing and beautiful book on this battle which we are about to celebrate the 700th anniversary of. I highly recommend it and encourage everyone who loves history to take a moment and purchase it."

Jason Shepherd

"Reading Harry Pearson's fine book, 'Clash of Crowns', took me back to the best history lessons at school. Harry clearly loves his subject, and his enthusiasm is infectious. But I am also struck by the depth and breadth of his knowledge. I found it a fascinating read, and wanted to get back to it again and again to discover the next instalment of a story of which I was largely ignorant. For me, it's a page turner."

Stephen Thompson

"I recently got this book and read it immediately from cover to cover, its an expertly and thoroughly researched book on a much undermined event, with an easy to read and understandable format.

The author covers the campaigns and pre-battle story but then fulfils its title by showing in great detail how and where the battle took place on that beautiful landscape in North Yorkshire... a must have for any devotee of British battles but also if you are a Yorkshireman and proud of your local history, but sometimes forgotten history."

Chris Rock

"Curious to know more about this fight in the war for Scottish independence? Then check out Harry Pearson's new title "Clash of

Foreword

As a child I was so fortunate that my grandparents lived in Northallerton and liked to visit the many historical sites in the region. My favourite was undoubtedly Byland Abbey, though Rievaulx came a close second. For my grandfather the area meant a great deal as he joined the King's Royal Rifles in 1915 in Helmsley, and was first billeted above a cobbler's shop in the town whilst training in Duncombe Park, the seat of his battalion commander, the Earl of Feversham, who was killed at the battle of Flers-Courcelette on 15 September 1916. I attended a number of First World War reunions with my grandfather in Helmsley.

There can be no doubt that this part of North Yorkshire is full of history – and full of evidence of the impact of history on both built and rural landscapes. The battle of Byland on 14 October 1322 has until now been neglected as both an event and a site. When visiting the area today it is hard to imagine thousands of English and Scottish troops engaged in bitter conflict there. The encounter was an important Scottish victory, since it emphasised the continuing military ascendancy of the Scots which had been so emphatically demonstrated at Bannockburn eight years earlier. Byland gave a further boost to the cause of Scottish independence. The battle stands out as a vibrant example of Scottish strength and determination, being fought so far south into England by a Scottish army pursuing a retreating English invasion force. Both kings were present – Edward II and Robert the Bruce – but it was the latter who demonstrated his skill as a tactician by sending troops up the precipitous slopes out of sight of the English, thereby encircling and routing the English army. Harry Pearson's book is both timely and welcome, with the 700th anniversary of the battle fast approaching, and I congratulate him for it. The battle has been in need of focused and careful analysis by someone with the necessary knowledge and understanding of the terrain. Supported by attractive illustrations and helpful maps, Harry has given the battle its rightful place in history, and also made strides in finding its rightful place on the ground, since this is a battle whose site has been disputed. Readers will also be grateful for the historical and military background Harry provides. And now there is another reason to visit this remarkable and attractive area of North Yorkshire, to retrace the steps of those who fought there through the battlefield walks which he has devised.

Anne Curry, Emeritus Professor of Medieval History,
University of Southampton

Chapter 1

The historical context – the Kingdoms of Scotland and England

At first glance it is tempting to think of the Battle of Byland as just another event in the seemingly constant warfare between the Kingdoms of England and Scotland throughout the medieval period, but this is a gross over-simplification and far from the truth. Indeed, while it is true to state that the invasion of Scotland by Edward I in 1296 set in train two and a half centuries of continual, if intermittent, Anglo-Scottish warfare, it is equally true that the preceding 200 years were marked by almost unbroken peace between the two nations.[1]

By the 11th century the two kingdoms of England and Scotland had evolved into approximately the countries we know today, and by and large they managed to co-exist peacefully up until the end of the 13th century. That is not to say that both nations did not endure strife during this period, each suffering episodes of attack, invasion and rebellion, but in terms of conflict between them, the instances were relatively few.

In the light of subsequent events, for the Scots the term 'the Auld Enemy' came to be synonymous with England, but prior to the 14th century the countries were anything but natural enemies. Each had greater and more pressing threats to their national interests. For Scotland it was the Kingdom of Norway, the Vikings, who for long periods exerted suzerainty over most of the Scottish islands, and attempted to extend that to parts of the mainland. In the case of England, successive French monarchs presented a persistent and serious threat to English territories in France.[2]

There were of course some occasional interruptions to this otherwise peaceful arrangement. In 1093 King Malcolm III was killed when fighting the English in Northumberland, and King David invaded England on several occasions to intervene on behalf of his niece the Empress Matilda during her civil war against King Stephen.

Malcolm's Cross, Alnwick, Northumberland. The inscription reads, 'Malcolm III King of Scotland, Beseiging Alnwick Castle, was slain here Nov. XIII AN MXCIII'. (Author)

Despite his defeat at the Battle of the Standard, which took place near Northallerton in 1138, David took advantage of the 'Anarchy' and internal strife to make significant inroads into England, and for a while it seemed that the three northern counties of England might be assimilated into the Kingdom of Scotland.

However, the balance of power tipped again, and once English unity had been restored under Henry II he forced David's successor, his 12-year old grandson Malcolm IV, by a combination of diplomacy and intimidation to surrender all the gains made by David. Malcolm's reign lasted only 12 years, and in 1165 he was succeeded by his altogether more warlike and ambitious brother, William (the Lion), who was determined to recover the disputed counties.[3] It was in pursuit of this aim that led to the impetuous William being captured by the English in the summer of 1174, whilst besieging Alnwick Castle in Northumberland. Henry refused to release William until he agreed the humiliating Treaty of Falaise, in which William acknowledged the English king as his feudal overlord, and allowed several key castles in Scotland to be garrisoned by English troops.

The fact that these were fairly isolated examples of hostilities serves to show that throughout the 11th, 12th and 13th centuries the prevailing characteristic of the relationship between the two countries was that of peaceful co-existence. It is worth noting that the few cases referred to were instances of Scottish incursions into England, and prior to the close of the 13th century, there had been no serious effort by England to invade Scotland,

Alnwick was attacked by the Scots on numerous occasions over the centuries. King William of Scotland was captured while laying siege to the castle in 1174. (Author)

let alone attempt conquest, and apart from these exceptions, relations between England and Scotland were largely peaceful and stable.[4]

The similarities between the two nations far outweighed the differences. True, Scotland had a strong 'Celtic fringe' in the north and west, but in lowland Scotland and the eastern coastal region where the bulk of the population and commerce was situated, there was little to distinguish them from their northern English neighbours in language, culture or religion.

Another powerful factor which fostered good relations between the countries was the strong dynastic links between the two royal houses, which was cemented by a series of marriages throughout the 12th and 13th centuries, including King Henry I to Matilda, sister of King Edgar (1100), Edgar's brother Prince David (later king David I) to Maud, Countess of Huntingdon (1113), and William the Lion to Ermengarde de Beaumont (1221).[5]

The future King David had been educated in England and spent many years at the English court, and after his sister Matilda's marriage to Henry, he became an influential protégé of the English King. David fully embraced Norman manners and customs, and saw great advantages in the feudal system as a model for ruling a kingdom and asserting royal authority, which he compared favourably with the more traditional, less centralised, and poorly organised arrangements that prevailed in his native Scotland.

So it was, when David ascended the throne of Scotland on the death of his brother Alexander I in 1124, that he began what has been described as 'a peaceful Norman Conquest of Scotland'.[6] Knights and barons who had been his companions at the court of Henry I were invited north of the border to settle, as he began the process of establishing the great Anglo-Norman families in Scotland.

It is at this time that some of the names that were subsequently to play pivotal roles in Scottish history first appear, notably Robert de Brus, who was granted 200,000 acres in Annandale. Brus' father had arrived in England with the Conqueror in 1066, and it is from him that the warrior king Robert the Bruce, so central to our story, was descended. These names include Walter Fitz-Alan, third son of a Breton knight, created hereditary High Steward of Scotland by David, and who became the antecedent of the royal house of Stewart, and others such as de Balliol, Comyn and Umphraville. Norman influence gradually spread throughout the whole island of Britain, from the south to the north.

The early Plantagenet kings continued to keep Scotland close through marriage alliances such as that arranged by King John of his daughter Princess Joan to King Alexander II of Scotland in 1221. Similarly, 30 years later Henry III oversaw the wedding of his daughter Margaret to Alexander III in York amidst great celebrations.[7]

This last royal marriage in 1251 marked a high-point in the close dynastic ties which had underpinned 200 years of Anglo-Scottish relations, with two stable and independent kingdoms, within well-established and recognised borders, with a largely common culture, and sharing the same Anglo-Norman ruling class.

Yet within 45 years we find the two countries engaged in full-scale war with England embarked on a brutal invasion of conquest, aimed at the destruction of an independent Scottish nation and its complete assimilation under English rule. What occasioned this complete transformation in the relationship between the two nations? What force brought about such political upheaval, leading to almost three centuries of conflict and warfare? The answer can be found in an unfortunate, indeed catastrophic from a Scottish viewpoint, alignment of circumstances – the development of a dynastic crisis in the succession to the Scottish throne, combined with the character and ambition of one man, Edward I, King of England.

View of York Minster. (CC MatzeTrier)

Lanercost Priory. Founded in 1166, this Augustinian monastery provides through its chronicler an excellent account of the Scottish wars. (Author)

Chapter 2

A dynastic crisis

The 13th century is often viewed by historians as something of a 'golden age' in Scotland's history, and certainly the country was transformed during the reigns of Alexander II (1214 – 49), and Alexander III (1249 – 86).[1] At the beginning of the century royal authority in Scotland was sparse and tenuous outside the central belt and east, with much of the country controlled by semi-autonomous magnates, or by the Norse kings who held sway in the islands of the west.

Alexander II extended royal power by force of arms into Argyll and Galloway, and his son and successor Alexander III consolidated these gains and increased them further by defeating the Vikings under King Haakon IV of Norway at the Battle of Largs in 1263, thereby ending their 500-year history of depredations in Scotland.[2] By the close of Alexander III's reign he ruled over a country with a centralised government in which the king's writ carried to every corner of the land.

This extension of 'the King's peace' coincided with, or perhaps fostered, a growing sense of national identity. The French-speaking baron, the English-speaking traders and merchants, the bishop who wrote in Latin, and the Gaelic-speaking clansmen of the Highlands and Galloway, all began to regard themselves as Scots, as part of something bigger than themselves or their own narrow community.[3] It was the burgeoning of a nation, and this sense of nationhood was soon to be enhanced and consolidated, ironically, by the aggression of successive English kings.

The stability and relative peace that derived from the expansion of royal authority set the conditions that fostered progress across many facets of Scottish society. The importation of feudalism, begun by David I and consolidated under the Alexanders, established the structure of a common law, a common church and, to a large extent, a common language across the kingdom.

The Great Seal of Alexander II, King of Scots (The Pictorial History of Scotland, 1859).

The law applied to all men, and derived from the King, and although much of the administration of justice was devolved to the feudal magnates and their tenants, royal power and authority was upheld by the *Justiciars,* one for the north and one for the south, who travelled the country to preside over the working of the law.

The Church in Scotland also flourished at this time, and with the support of David and successive kings managed to resist attempts by the sees of York and Canterbury to assert English authority over it. This was confirmed by Pope Celestine III in 1192 by his bull *Cum universi,* which declared the Scottish church to be the 'special daughter of Rome'.

During the 12th and 13th centuries the diocesan system was fully established and many of the 'new' religious orders founded institutions in Scotland, including the Benedictines (Dunfermline), the Cistercians (Melrose), the Premonstratensians (Dryburgh), and the Cluniacs (Paisley). The abbeys and monasteries not only stimulated the spiritual life of Scottish society, but also influenced the economic and cultural development of the community. They introduced new building techniques and architectural styles as witnessed by the great cathedrals such as Glasgow and St. Andrews, and contributed greatly to commerce through agriculture, mining and the wool trade.

This economic prosperity was mirrored in secular society through the growth of the Royal Burghs, the first real towns to appear in Scotland. These evolved from forts or fortified settlements, and under royal patronage sprang up across Scotland in places such as Edinburgh, Berwick, Roxburgh and Stirling. Successive kings facilitated their growth through measures such as the minting of a regulated silver coinage and encouraging foreign merchants and craftsmen to settle in the new centres of trade and commerce. The Burghs were granted privileges and some measure of self-government by the Crown, and enjoyed the protection of the King's Chamberlain, who appointed sheriffs to look after their interests.

It is around this time that the form of northern English known as *Scots* began to assume hegemony as the language of trade and business, and by the end of the 13th century had largely ousted both French, the language of the aristocracy, and Gaelic, the language of the peasant, as the common tongue of Scotland.

Although coming relatively late to Scotland, the great European urban and commercial development of the High Middle Ages, and the international trade and cultural interaction it fostered, allowed individual Scots to make their mark on a wider stage. Men such as Baldred Bisset, who achieved an international reputation as among the foremost lawyers of his day, and John Duns Scotus, regarded as one of the most important and influential philosopher-theologians in Christendom, are examples of Scotland's high standing at the close of the 13th century.

It was a time of progress on a number of fronts: political, economical, and intellectual, all underpinned by the rule of a competent and shrewd king who understood the importance of peaceful relations with his powerful southern neighbour. Protected against foreign enemies, and securely established at home, the royal house of Dunkeld had flourished and was firmly rooted in power, but it had a fatal weakness in the lack of a direct successor to the throne.

The Scottish philosopher-theologian John Duns Scotus was one of the most influential thinkers of the High Middle Ages. (Galleria Nazionale delle Marche)

It was a problem that had plagued several generations of the royal dynasty. Alexander II had so despaired of a legitimate successor that he named his second cousin Robert de Brus as heir presumptive, before producing a male heir late in his reign, who was to become Alexander III as an eight-year-old in 1249.

For a while it had all looked so promising for Alexander. He had married Princess Margaret of England, daughter of Henry III, amid much pomp and ceremony at York on 26th December 1251, when he was ten years old and she eleven. Eventually they produced three children, before Margaret died in 1275, namely, Margaret (b. 1261), Alexander (b.1264), and David (b.1272). Tragically all three predeceased their father, dying within three years of each other, and when Prince Alexander died in 1284, the King found himself both a widower and without a son to succeed to the throne.[4]

Alexander did have a legitimate heir, the 9-month-old Princess Margaret of Norway, known to history as 'the Maid of Norway'.

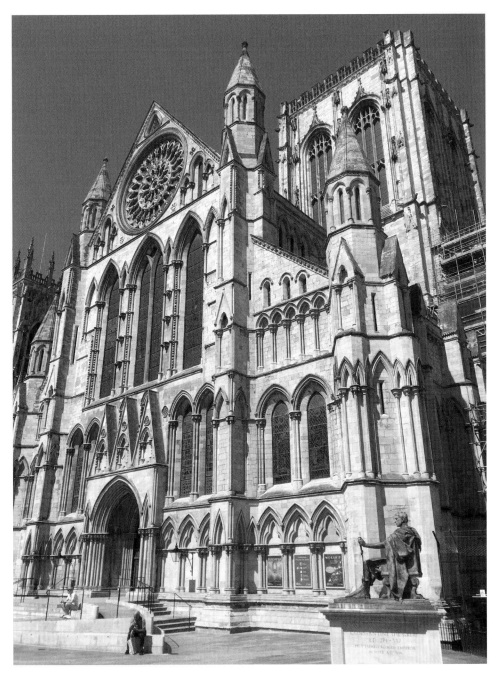

On St. Stephen's Day 1251, Archbishop Walter de Fray conducted the marriage of the 10-year-old King Alexander III of Scotland to his 11-year-old bride Princess Margaret of England in the recently completed South Transept of York Minster. (Author)

Alexander's daughter Margaret had married King Eric II of Norway in 1281, and their daughter 'the Maid', was born in April 1283. Her mother tragically, if not uncommonly, died in childbirth.

In terms of medieval kingship, the fact that the heir presumptive was both a girl and an infant was a dangerous situation, but as Alexander

Statue of Alexander III on the west door of St.Giles', Edinburgh. (Kim Traynor)

was only 43 and regarded as still in his prime, the circumstances were not yet critical. He wasted no time in remarrying, and chose Yolande de Dreux, a young French noble woman and noted beauty, as his new consort, and Alexander and Yolande were married on the 14th of October 1285 in a ceremony at Jedburgh Abbey, attended by a great assembly of the Scottish and French nobility.

In many ways Yolande was an ideal choice of bride for the Scottish king, and his desire to secure and strengthen his dynasty. At the time of their marriage Yolande was, at 22, of prime child-bearing age and in robust health. She was the daughter of Robert IV, Count of Dreux and his wife Beatrice, Countess of Montfort, and thus a scion of the House of Capetian, one of the most ancient and distinguished royal houses of Europe. There was great optimism that further male heirs would follow in due course, but sadly for Alexander and his new queen, and for Scotland, this proved not to be the case.

The calamity occurred on a dark March night in 1286. The King had spent the day in conference with the lords of his council at Edinburgh Castle, and according to the Lanercost Chronicle, their deliberations had been followed by much feasting and drinking.[5] Although the hour had grown late, and no doubt emboldened by wine, the King decided to journey to join his new queen, who he had left at the royal manor of Kinghorn, some 20 miles from Edinburgh on the far side of the Firth of Forth. It was a wild and stormy night, and the King's courtiers tried in vain to dissuade him from travelling in such inclement weather. Refusing all counsel to the contrary, he mounted his horse and set off for the ferry at Dalmeny, accompanied only by three squires.

On reaching the far shore at Inverkeithing he was met by a member of his household who beseeched him to travel no further in the treacherous conditions, but the King was determined to reach the royal bed that night, and calling for a local guide set off with his escort along the shore road to Kinghorn. Somewhere on the way the party became separated, and the next morning the lifeless body of the King was found at the foot of the cliffs where his horsed had stumbled in the darkness.[6]

In an instant Scotland was no longer ruled by a strong, shrewd and capable king, but by a 3-year-old motherless girl on the far side of the North Sea, and the immediate result was the creation of a power vacuum around the throne. This represented a temptation that was to prove irresistible to the powerful and opportunistic neighbour to the south, Edward I.

Edward I, one of England's ablest kings of the medieval era. (© Dulwich Picture Gallery)

Chapter 3

'Malleus Scotorum'

It was a particularly unfortunate circumstance for Scotland, that this unprecedented crisis in national affairs coincided with the reign of one of England's most competent, ambitious, and ruthless kings, Edward Plantagenet. His tomb in Westminster Abbey bears the inscription 'Scotorum Malleus' - 'Hammer of the Scots', but at the time of Alexander's death in 1286 Edward had not yet earned that fearsome epithet.

Edward I was a remarkable monarch by any standards, and perhaps the outstanding English king of the medieval era. During his reign the foundations of an organised legislature and the parliamentary system were laid, the balance of power between church and crown realigned in favour of the lay authority, and the system of feudal levies restructured into an organised and powerful military force.[1]

In his appearance and bearing he was every inch a king, tall (at over 6 feet almost regarded as a giant in his day, earning him his nickname 'Longshanks'), handsome and athletic. He was devout in his religious observations, and sober and unpretentious in his demeanour. One of the foremost captains of the age, he was a renowned soldier and fearless in battle, and as a contemporary wrote - *"He is valiant as a lion, quick to attack the strongest and fearing the onslaught of none."*[2]

In an age when monarchs were not known for their constancy, Edward placed great store on honesty and integrity. His motto was 'Pactum Serva' (Keep troth), and he was single-minded in doing what was right, as he understood it. However, this admirable quality was coupled with a very subjective, indeed blinkered viewpoint, a tendency to interpret all circumstances to his own advantage, and an unswerving belief in the righteousness of his actions.

This, then, was the man that fate decreed would have a momentous and far-reaching impact on Scottish affairs. If Alexander III had found

The tomb of Edward I in Westminster Abbey – 'Malleus Scotorum' – 'the Hammer of the Scots'. (© Dean and Chapter of Westminster Abbey)

him to be a reliable and staunch friend, his successors were to inherit an implacable and merciless enemy.

Hitherto Edward had always seemed well-disposed towards Scotland. King Alexander and his English queen Margaret had attended Edward's coronation, and were regular visitors to the English court. Edward referred to Alexander as his "beloved brother",[3] and it was convenient for him to know that when he was engaged in war and adventures in France and Wales that he had a friend on his northern border. With the death of Alexander that sense of security was lost, and Edward turned his mind to ways to re-establish it and make it stronger, and he found what seemed to be the perfect solution – a marriage between the infant Queen Margaret and his own son and heir, Edward of Caernarfon (later to succeed as Edward II).

This opportunity that now presented itself fitted well with Edward's long-held ambitions. To him it was incongruous that the island of Britain should be separated into 3 distinct countries, each with its own ruler and laws. He saw himself as the legitimate successor to the fabled King Arthur of antiquity, and like his semi-mythical predecessor, rightful ruler of all of Britain.[4] By the time of Alexander's death Edward was already King of England and Ireland, Duke of Aquitaine, and master of the recently-subdued Wales, and only the weakened and vulnerable Kingdom of Scotland stood between him and his cherished aim to rule over the entire British Isles.

A dynastic marriage between 3-year-old Margaret and 2-year-old Edward would give the English King immediate 'de facto' control over Scotland, and in the space of a generation join the two countries together in the personal union of a single monarch, a full 300 years before James I and VI brought that about in 1603.

A proposal along those lines was therefore put to the 'Guardians', a Council of Regency consisting of 6 nobles and prelates appointed to rule Scotland in the name of the young queen. For their part the Guardians, aware of the mutual benefits of peace between the two nations, and conscious of the fact that many of the Scottish nobility held lands in both Scotland and England, were amenable to such an arrangement, provided the ancient liberties of Scotland were safeguarded, and so according to Tytler, *"It was agreed by the English plenipotentiaries that the rights, laws, liberties, and customs of Scotland were to be inviolably observed in all time coming, throughout the whole kingdom and its marches,..."*[5]

The matter was formally concluded by representatives

Edward of Caernarfon created Prince of Wales by his father Edward I. (© British Library)

of Scotland, Norway, and England in the Treaty of Birgham-on-Tweed in 1290, and the issue appeared settled to the mutual advantage of all parties. In addition to agreeing the marriage of Queen Margaret to Prince Edward, the main articles of the treaty declared that -

- The Kingdom of Scotland was forever to remain undivided and separate from England, free in itself and without subjection.
- Should Margaret and Edward, or either of them (from any subsequent marriage) fail to produce an heir, the kingdom should revert to the nearest legitimate heir.
- Should Margaret survive her husband she should be returned to Scotland free from any matrimonial commitments.
- The Scottish Church was to remain free from English jurisdiction and control.
- No native of Scotland could be compelled to answer to an English court on any civil or criminal matter alleged to have taken place in Scotland.[6]

It is interesting to note that under the terms relating to succession it would appear that Prince Edward would gain a personal right to the Scottish crown should Margaret predecease him childless, and that the inheritance could pass to his heirs by another wife. It is not clear if the Scottish commissioners agreed with that interpretation, but as events transpired it was never put to the test.

Just as a peaceful and equitable resolution seemed to have been achieved, disaster struck yet again in the most ill-fated of circumstances. When Margaret first became Queen, her father, King Eric II of Norway, felt she was too young to undertake the hazardous journey across the North Sea, and it was decided that she would remain with her father until such time as she was old enough to withstand the rigours of travel, and when matters in Scotland were more settled. However once the Treaty of Birgham was agreed, it was deemed expedient that she should be brought to Scotland so that arrangements for the marriage could proceed. Unfortunately the young Queen fell ill on the voyage, and died in Orkney on the 26th of September 1290, without ever laying eyes on her realm.

The death of the young Queen marks a watershed in Edward's relations with Scotland. Hitherto he had been content to take advantage

Edward I, from the Choir Screen at York Minster. (Author)

of the unusual circumstances which had arisen, which seemed destined to facilitate the realisation of his greatest ambition – to extend the supremacy of the English crown over the northern kingdom. Now those plans lay in tatters, and all of Edward's diplomacy, manoeuvring and scheming came to nought. Faced with the new situation, a new strategy was called for, one which was less subtle and amenable, and one where English might and power was more nakedly displayed.[7]

In Scotland the state of affairs was now critical. With no obvious or direct claimant to the throne, various candidates put themselves forward and sought to advance their claims by diplomatic and/or warlike means. Civil war threatened, and a the prospect of a return to the anarchy that had so often plaqued Scotland in the past loomed large. Alarmed at this danger, some of the leading men of the nation looked to Edward to intervene, as the only power available capable of imposing order. No fewer than thirteen candidates had declared their right to the throne, but it soon became clear that two of them had particularly strong claims – John Balliol and Robert Bruce (grandfather of King Robert the Bruce who was to fight at Byland).[8]

Both were descended from Prince David, younger brother of William I 'the Lion'. John Balliol was Lord of Galloway through his mother Devorguilla (who founded Balliol College Oxford in 1250), whose lineage sprang from David's eldest daughter, Margaret.

Robert Bruce, 5th Lord of Annandale, (known to history as 'the Competitor' to distinguish him from his illustrious grandson) based his claim on his descent from Isabella, second daughter of Prince David, and on the fact that his second cousin Alexander II had named him as his successor before producing heirs of his own. His case was strengthened by the fact that he had also acted as Regent of Scotland in the minority of Alexander III.

Both had a strong claim to the throne and many adherents to promote their cause. Bishop Fraser of St. Andrews wrote to King Edward in support of Balliol and urged him to move to the border in force to overawe the protagonists and prevent bloodshed. To counter this, seven senior Earls who favoured Bruce appealed to Edward to intervene and invited him to arbitrate in the dispute.

It is unclear if the Council of Regency ever formally invited Edward to adjudicate in the question of the succession, but when he made known his willingness to do so, his offer was readily accepted. After all, he had a reputation for integrity and impartiality, was known as a skilled jurist, and in the recent marriage negotiations had shown himself careful of the ancient rights and privileges of Scotland. Little did the Scots know they were inviting a wolf into the fold.

Whether this represented naivety or lack of judgement on behalf of the Scots meant little to Edward, and he determined to take full advantage of their weakness. In May 1291 he took up residence at Norham Castle on the border, and summoned his army to join him. The leading men of Scotland and the various competitors were called before him, and through his Chief Justice he informed them he was acting in the matter, not as an impartial friend and arbitrator, but as the rightful feudal overlord of Scotland, styling himself 'Lord Paramount of Scotland' in the process.

The Scots were completely surprised by this development, and taken aback as the wolf cast off his sheep's clothing. Playing for time, they asked for proceedings to be postponed to consider their position. Edward gave them twenty four hours, and when they complained that was insufficient, granted a further three weeks, knowing that by that time his army would be assembled around him.

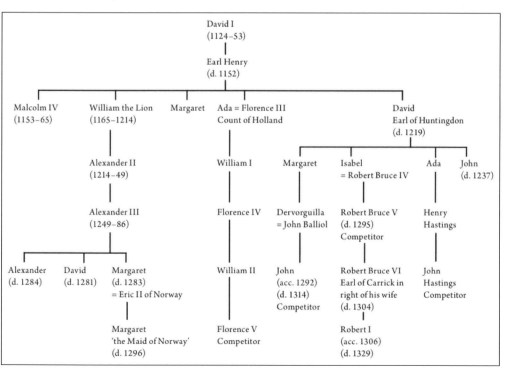

The Scottish Royal Succession and claimants to the throne.

Edward's claim to suzerainty was flimsy to say the least. It was based on some vague antecedents in earlier centuries, when the princes of northern Britain had expressed a form of fealty to the Anglo-Saxon rulers in the south, and, more recently, on the Treaty of Falaise in 1174, in which King William I 'the Lion' had accepted the overlordship of Henry II in exchange for his freedom.

When the Scots demurred at this, and pointed out that in 1189 Richard I 'Coeur de Lion' had nullified the terms of the Falaise agreement in exchange for a hefty sum,[9] Edward brushed aside their objections and demanded that his overlordship be recognised by all, and that each of the competitors must swear allegiance to him before he would consider their claim.

Resistance was not only futile, but impossible. Edward was poised on the border with a formidable army, and the barely-disguised threat to use force should anyone attempt to defy him. Having been so long at peace, Scotland was hopelessly unprepared for war, and her leading men bitterly divided as to who should ascend the empty throne. One by one the Competitors swore fealty to the English King, and shortly afterwards the 'Guardians' handed over custody of the realm, and agreed to admit English garrisons to the main royal castles.

With Scotland in the palm of his hand, without a blow needing to be struck, Edward now proceeded to judgement among the claimants, which quickly came down to a choice between Balliol and Bruce. At first glance, and by modern standards, it would seem that Balliol had the best claim, being descended from a more senior line than Bruce. However in those days primogeniture was by no means the accepted norm of succession in Scotland. Bruce was a nearer descendant in terms of generations, had previously been designated as heir presumptive, and had the support of 'the Seven Earls', who, by ancient right and tradition had the authority to elect the king.

At first Edward leaned towards Bruce, his old comrade-in-arms and fellow crusader, but, according to Fordun, was persuded against that choice because Bruce, although by that time in his eighties, was a 'strong man', and Balliol, a man of less resolute character, might be more amenable to Edward's 'influence'.[10]

In the end, on the 17th of November 1292, Edward decided in favour of Balliol, a perfectly legitimate choice from a strictly legalistic standpoint, although entirely opportunistic and advantageous for the English king. The new King John was crowned King of Scots at Scone on the 30th of

King John Balliol paying homage to Edward I. (© British Library)

November, and as such paid homage to King Edward as his liege man on the 26th of December. By accepting Edward's overlordship, King John had reduced himself to the level of an ordinary vassal and his kingdom to that of a feudal holding. He did not have to wait long for that to be made humiliatingly obvious.

In January 1293, under pressure from Edward, John was forced to issue an instrument declaring the Treaty of Birgham null and void,[11] thus releasing Edward from '*every article, concession or promise*' pertaining to the ancient rights and privileges of Scotland protected by that document, including the guarantee that Scottish legal disputes should only be heard by Scottish courts.[12] Once John surrendered these rights, he was lost.

Edward missed no opportunity to humiliate Balliol and debase his kingly authority. Time and time again he was summoned to Westminster to appear in person like a common defendant to respond to charges brought by various plaintiffs, even on one occasion to answer why he had not paid his wine merchant's bill.[13]

If Scotland's puppet king was able to tolerate these calculated insults, the nation as a whole found it increasingly difficult to do so. John was labelled 'Toom Tabard' (meaning 'Empty Coat') for his obsequious and compliant behaviour, and anti-English sentiment festered and grew.

Matters came to a head in 1294 when Edward summoned Balliol to London yet again, this time to demand money and men for an impending campaign against France. The English king held vast lands in France as Duke of Aquitane, in which capacity he was a feudal vassal of the King of France. Edward had indeed paid homage to King Philip IV ('the Fair') in 1286, soon after the latter had ascended the throne, but when summoned again to the French court in 1293 to answer for the capture of French ships and the sacking of La Rochelle by English sailors, Edward refused to do so.

In response to this act of defiance Philip declared Edward's vast territories in Gascony forfeit, and as a result Edward prepared for war, hence his demand that Balliol provide financial and military support. The great irony in this situation is that Edward expected the same degree of obedience, fealty and homage from Balliol that he himself refused to Philip, his own feudal overlord in France.

This was a step too far for the Scots who, meeting in Parliament at Scone, rejected Edward's demands and instead sent ambassadors to France to conclude a treaty with the French king against the English. This belated act of defiance served only to enrage Edward and invite retribution, and it was only the need to deal with rebellion in Wales that prevented an immediate invasion. However the reckoning was merely delayed not avoided, and having crushed the Welsh with great severity in 1295, Edward turned his attention to Scotland. The English levies were summoned to Newcastle by the 1st of March 1296, and a great fleet assembled to supply them by sea on the march up the coast.

The whole fury of Edward now fell on Scotland. Crossing the Tweed he appeared before Berwick, which like most Scottish towns was unwalled, and protected only by a shallow ditch and a wooden palisade. The English men-at-arms made short work of the flimsy defences, sweeping aside all resistance. Edward was determined to make an example of Berwick, and gave the town over to be sacked by his soldiers. For three days the slaughter and pillage raged unabated, as the entire population of Berwick, man, woman and child, was put to the sword. Estimates range from 4,000 to 17,000 who perished in an act of barbarity unparalleled in the history of this island.

King Edward was determined that Berwick would be annexed into the realm of England, and remained at Berwick to supervise the construction of new and massive defences. The entire town as it then stood was encompassed by a strong stone wall 22 feet (6.7m) high and 3 feet 4 inches (1m) thick, stretching some 2 miles long from end to end. The pre-existing castle on the north-west corner of the enclosure

An English man-at-arms, representing John de Warenne, 6th Earl of Surrey, who defeated the Scots at Dunbar in 1296 and was appointed Viceroy of Scotland by Edward I. (Dean Davidson © 3 Swords Historical Services)

was also rebuilt and strengthened.[14] So effective were the new defences that the Scots, who had recaptured the town in 1318 by stealth and subterfuge, were able to withstand a sustained siege by a powerful and well-equipped English army in September 1319.

Meanwhile the English army, under the command of John de Warenne 6th Earl of Surrey, had moved north to besiege Dunbar Castle. A large but inexperienced Scottish army attempted to lift the siege, but was utterly routed by Surrey on 27th of April with great loss. Thereupon the garrison at Dunbar promptly surrendered, and in effect any serious military opposition to Edward was at an end.

The remainder of his campaign in Scotland was something of a procession. Castle after castle yielded without a blow being struck, or after a mere token resistance. Roxburgh, Dumbarton, Jedburgh, Stirling and Edinburgh fell in quick succession. By June Edward had reached Perth which opened its gates before him, and there he received a letter from Balliol begging for peace and offering abject surrender.

Two weeks later at Montrose, the puppet king appeared before his master to formally surrender his 'kingdom' and, after being publicly and humiliatingly stripped of the tokens of kingship, was despatched to confinement in the Tower of London.[15] Edward continued his now leisurely progress north, and by the end of the month had reached Elgin on the Moray Firth. No foreign invader had penetrated so deep into Scotland since Julius Agricola carried the Roman eagles north of the Grampians in the first century, and the entire country lay prostrate at Edward's feet.

Not content with military conquest, the English king set about stripping Scotland of every vestige of national identity. The Stone of Destiny, the sacred relic on which kings of Scotland were traditionally enthroned was removed to Westminster, together with the royal regalia and archives. The message was clear – Scotland was no longer an independent nation, but a personal possession of the English monarch.

On his way back to England at the end of August he held a parliament at Berwick, and every landowner in Scotland was summoned to swear fealty to Edward personally. A new government for Scotland was laid out, similar to that which had been imposed on conquered Wales. The Earl of Surrey was made Governor, with Hugh de Cressingham as his

Statue of William Wallace at Edinburgh Castle. (Author)

avaricious Treasurer, who appointed a host of civil servants and clerks to ensure the new fiefdom could be efficiently and profitably taxed. English priests were appointed to positions in the Church, and English garrisons held the castles.[16]

Edward had every reason to feel self-satisfied. All he had strived for had come to pass, and his long-held ambition of a Britain united under his rule had been realised by a combination of guile and brute force. However, as he was soon to discover, his arrogant, heavy-handed and tactless treatment of Scotland served only to inflame the sense of national sentiment it was designed to eradicate.[17]

Chapter 4

Resistance and Subjugation

Although most of the nobility and ruling class of Scotland was cowed, imprisoned, or indeed in the service of the English king, the spirit of resistance continued through the lesser gentry, the small land-holders, the townspeople and peasants, and within a year this resistance had become outright rebellion against the rapacious and corrupt regime of occupation.

The revolt against English rule had ignited spontaneously and independently in different parts of the country, in the north under Sir Andrew de Moray, a high-ranking knight who had fought at Dunbar in 1296, and in the south led by William Wallace, whose name was to become synonymous with the struggle for independence. These two brave and enterprising leaders led their men in daring escapades against the occupying forces. English patrols were ambushed, outposts overrun, castles retaken, and with each success more men flocked to join them.

Whilst the character of Wallace looms large in the popular consciousness of this period, that of Andrew Moray has been somewhat overlooked in comparison. This is due in the main to Wallace's career being the subject of a popular 15th century epic poem *'The Wallace'* by the minstrel 'Blind Harry', and his well-documented trial and brutal execution at the hands of Edward I in 1305 which cemented his status as a martyr to the cause of Scottish freedom.

By contrast little is known about the death of Moray, but circumstantial evidence suggests he was mortally wounded at the Battle of Stirling Bridge and died some months later. Despite the disparity in their respective reputations, many historians now believe that Moray was more likely to be the leading figure in their partnership, based on social standing, training and experience.

Probably born around 1270 (exact date unknown) Moray was the oldest son of one of the most important barons in the north-east of

Scotland, Sir Andrew Moray of Petty. As such he would have received the education and military training of one destined for a prominent role in both local and national affairs. Wallace on the other hand was the younger son of a minor knight from Elderslie in Renfrewshire. Born in 1272, local legend claims he was educated by the monks at the nearby Paisley Abbey, and his early reputation was that of an outlaw and resistance fighter rather than a leader in a conventional military sense.

Moray and his father fought in the Scottish army that was defeated by the Earl of Surrey at Dunbar, and both were captured and incarcerated, the father in the Tower of London with other principal prisoners, and the son in Chester Castle. Moray did not remain in confinement long, and at some point over the winter of 1296-97 he escaped from his captivity and made his way back to his father's lands in the north-east, appearing in arms there at Avoch Castle in May 1297.

We do not hear of William Wallace in opposition to the English until his raid on Lanark in that same month, when an affray at Lanark resulted in Wallace and his followers killing William de Heselrig the English Sheriff of Lanark, and burning several houses. Certainly at this point in time King Edward regarded Moray's rebellion as a much more serious threat than Wallace's more guerilla-type insurrection.

Moray raised a significant and organised military force which campaigned across the north-east of Scotland, laying siege to Urquhart Castle (unsuccessfully), before attacking and capturing Duffus Castle, which had been held for the King by Sir Reginald Cheyne. In response Edward sent a strong force north under the Earl of Buchan to confront Moray, but after a stand-off in Speyside, Sir Andrew was able to evade the stronger force without giving battle.

When, in early September 1297, Moray and Wallace managed to combine their forces in order to lay siege to the important fortress of Dundee Castle, it is likely that the former was able to bring a body of troops that was greater in numbers, better organised and better armed than the contingent commanded by Wallace. This, together with Moray's superior rank, experience and training, is why many commentators considered it likely that, although the two men clearly agreed to share the responsibility of leadership, he was the senior figure in the partnership. This is also borne out by the fact that in two letters which they jointly sent in 1297, one on the 11th of October to the mayors of Hamburg and Lübeck, and another dated the 7th of November to the Prior of Hexham

Abbey, in both instances Sir Andrew is assigned primacy in the letters as sent from *"Andrew de Moray and William Wallace, leaders of the kingdom of Scotland and the community of the realm."*

Regardless of how their collaboration worked, or whom, if either, was the more effective leader, the fact was that between them they had rendered Scotland ungovernable for Edward and his officials, and their combined military strength was now a very real and dangerous threat to the English presence north of the border. Worse still from the English administration's point of view, taxes were not being collected.[1]

Finally the viceroy Surrey was stirred into action, and led a strong army of mounted knights and footmen north from Berwick to confront Moray and Wallace, who broke off their siege of Dundee Castle in order to meet this threat.

Both armies converged on the town of Stirling, whose strategic importance conferred upon it the title of 'the gateway to Scotland', and on the 11th of September 1297 met on either side of a bridge over the River Forth. The English commanders seemed contemptuous of their more

The 15th C. Old Stirling Bridge, built to replace the wooden structure which previously stood there, and site of Sir Andrew de Moray and William Wallace's victory of 1297.

lightly-armed opponents, or else oblivious to the danger of attempting to cross a river in the face of an enemy force, and ordered the army to cross over the bridge, so narrow as to only permit two to cross side by side.

The Scots, scarcely believing their luck, calmly waited until a large part the English had crossed over, then rushed forward to seize the bridge, thus trapping half of the army on the north side, isolated from their comrades who could only look on helplessly. The result was a slaughter which few escaped from. Among those slain was the hated Cressingham, of whom it is said the skin was flayed from his body to make gruesome souvenirs for the Scottish soldiers.[2]

Surrey fled in a panic to the border, leaving what remained of his army to fend for themselves in the face of the vengeful Scots. Wallace and Moray were now undisputed masters of Scotland, apart from some of the stronger castles where English garrisons still held out; however, within a few weeks Moray succumbed to wounds received in the battle. Wallace was now the sole 'Guardian of Scotland', and seizing the initiative, led a series of punitive raids to ravage and plunder the northern counties of England.

Meanwhile Edward, thinking that matters had been settled in Scotland, was engaged in a fairly ineffectual campaign in Flanders when news reached him of the disaster at Stirling Bridge. He managed to agree a two-year truce with the French king, before turning his attention once again to deal with the Scots. Levies were summoned from Gascony, Wales and Ireland, as well as from every corner of England, and the vast army that was mustered on the border on the 25th of June 1298 numbered some 2,500 heavy cavalry and 12,500 foot.

With around 6,000 infantry and a few hundred light horse, the Scots were hopelessly outnumbered. They fell back in the face of such an overwhelming force, refusing battle and wasting the land as they retreated in order to deny the English the means to supply their great host, and for a while it seemed those tactics might succeed.

By the 21st of July Edward had reached beyond Edinburgh without catching sight of the Scottish army. His men were starving and mutinous, and he was on the point of ordering a retreat when word reached him that Wallace and his men were only 13 miles away near Falkirk. Before the Scots were able to retreat further, Edward quickly advanced on their position and forced them to stand and fight. It was a battle that could only have one outcome.

Hitherto, Wallace's successes had been largely achieved by 'hit and run' and guerilla tactics, but he was not a general in the conventional sense. Now, with barely a third of their number, he faced one of the most formidable armies in Europe, commanded by the ablest captain of the age. The Scots had little but courage to offer in resistance, yet for a while this served them well. Their army consisted almost entirely of spearmen, and Wallace had organised them into 'schiltrons' - dense circular formations which presented an impenetrable barrier of steel on every side.[3]

Wave after wave of English cavalry broke on the wall of spears, to no avail and with heavy loss as the Scots stood firm. Having allowed chivalry its opportunity, Edward now turned to a more pragmatic and deadly course of action. Calling up his thousands of English and Welsh bowmen, he ordered them to turn their weapons on the densely packed Scottish formations. Volley after volley poured down on the defenceless spearmen, and soon their ranks were depleted and disorganised.

Once again Edward sent in the heavy cavalry, and this time they smashed through the weakened defences as the Scottish army fell apart. The rout became a slaughter, and although Wallace managed to escape into the nearby woods with a few surviving followers, his brief career as the leader of Scottish resistance was over. He remained at large as a fugitive for a further seven years, before his capture and brutal execution at the hands of a vengeful Edward's executioner in 1305.[4]

The figure of William Wallace remains somewhat controversial to this day, and the level of his achievements debated. A stark assessment can say that he achieved very little. His defeat at Falkirk left Scotland more firmly under English domination than when he instigated his revolt, with nothing to show for the great cost in Scottish lives lost in the struggle. Many commentators believe his single great success at Stirling Bridge was largely the work of his colleague Moray, a man trained in the art of war and with much greater experience of battle, but whose untimely death left Wallace with the plaudits.

What is undeniable, however, is that Wallace was a man of great courage and determination, and he kept the embers of resistance alive when they were all but extinguished. In some ways he achieved more in death than in life, and the cruel and vicious manner of his execution[5], premised on unjust charges, did more to foster a sense of Scottish national identity than even his feats on the battlefield.[6] Without Wallace, Scotland may well have gone the way of Ireland and Wales, subsumed under the English crown, and the whole history of Great Britain drastically altered. As it were, his brave, if ultimately futile resistance, was to lay the foundations for one greater to build on, namely Robert the Bruce.

With the destruction of the Scottish field army, the Battle of Falkirk left Edward once again master of Scotland, but quite apart from its immediate effect the battle is of significant importance in military history. Firstly, the determined resistance of the Scottish schiltrons demonstrated that well-organised and disciplined infantry could withstand assaults by heavy cavalry, and this lesson would be applied successfully in future conflicts, including Bannockburn.

Secondly, Edward's inspired tactical use of massed archers began an era of supremacy for the longbow which, when deployed effectively, made English armies irresistible for over 100 years. It heralded the end of the old, chivalric view of war, in which an elite military caste fought it out on horseback among themselves, according to knightly convention. Instead it marked the rise of the common soldier who, properly armed and trained, was more than a match for the knight on horseback.[7]

Despite his complete victory at Falkirk, Edward was unable to immediately subdue or pacify Scotland. There was widespread

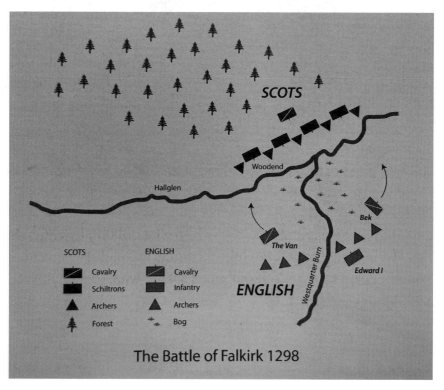

The Battle of Falkirk 1298.

Detail of King Robert Bruce's statue at Bannockburn. (Author)

resentment of English rule, inspired by a burgeoning sense of national identity which affected nobility and commoners alike. This sentiment, ironically, had largely been fostered by Edward's arrogant, heavy-handed and brutal methods, and no sooner was rebellion crushed in one quarter, when it arose elsewhere.

It was said that what was conquered in the summer was lost in the winter, and Edward had to mount a series of campaigns in an attempt to consolidate his position. In 1301, 1303 and 1304 he led vast punitive expeditions north, and on two occasions defied the conventions of medieval warfare by over-wintering on campaign.

Finally his perseverance began to pay dividends, and one by one his principle opponents, wearied by war and worn down by Edward's implacable determination, came to terms and acknowledged his overlordship. One of those who reached accommodation was Robert Bruce, who on his father's death in 1304 became Earl of Carrick and Lord of Annandale, with vast lands on both sides of the border, including in Essex and Huntingdon. Bruce was grandson of Robert Bruce 'the Competitor', and from him also inherited a legitimate claim to the throne of Scotland.[8]

Chapter 5

'Cometh the hour, cometh the man' – Robert Bruce

Like most of the Scottish magnates, Bruce had fought for and against King Edward in the confused and troubled times of recent years, his path mostly determined by his family's fierce enmity with the house of Balliol and their Comyn kinsmen, and on succeeding his father at the age of thirty was already a seasoned warrior, diplomat and politician.

Since his surrender to Edward in 1302 he had trod a delicate path, attempting to pay outward allegiance to the English king, while studiously avoiding rendering any significant military service which might assist him in his attempts to subjugate Scotland. All the while Bruce was quietly and steadily preparing for the time when he would assert his claim to the Crown of Scotland, and take his rightful place on the throne.[1] Ever the pragmatist, he recognised in Edward I a dangerous obstacle to his ambitions, and therefore all his planning was predicated on the death of this formidable monarch, who was now in his mid 60s and showing signs of ailing. A lifetime of hard soldiering had taken its toll, and successive winter campaigns in Scotland had worn him out. Bruce could afford to be patient, but events were soon to overtake his cautious designs.

In October 1305 Edward lay in his sickbed, and with rumours abounding of his imminent demise, the leading figures in Scotland looked to how they might use his death to throw off the English yoke. Apart from Bruce, the other 'strong man' in Scottish affairs at that time was John Comyn 'the Red', Lord of Badenoch, scion of the house of Balliol, and therefore natural enemy of Bruce. Both men had been induced by the leading figures of the Scottish church, Bishops Wishart and Lamberton, to set aside their ancestral enmity, and enter into a sealed bond to join forces against the English when the moment was right.

According to the chronicler Walter Bower, Bruce put a proposal to Comyn, that either he (Bruce) would help Comyn to become king, in exchange for all of Comyn's lands, or Comyn should have all the Bruce territory if he should assist Bruce to the throne -

> *"...although by right and by the customs and laws of the country the honour of the royal dignity and the succession to it...were recognised as belonging to him (Bruce) in preference to any others, yet...he made an offer to the said John (Comyn) to choose one of two alternatives – either to reign and assume to himself the entire government of the kingdom...while granting to the same Robert all his lands and possessions, or to assume perpetual rights over all the lands and possessions of the said Robert for himself... leaving to the same Robert the kingdom and the kingly honour..."*[2]

Comyn chose the latter proposition, and the pair exchanged written undertakings and oaths to mutually bind them to the agreement. However, for a reason unknown, perhaps because word had come that Edward had recovered his vigour, or because he saw it as an opportunity to be finally free of his bitter rival, Comyn decided to betray Bruce, and reveal the plot to the King.

> *"By his messages and private letters to the King of England he (Comyn) shamelessly gave away Robert's own secrets... thinking that with Robert de Bruce out of the way, he himself might without difficulty gain control of all Scotland with the assent of the King of England."*[3]

Other chroniclers corroborate Bower's account, but have Comyn as the instigator, but either way it is clear a bond was entered into, which Comyn chose to betray.[4,5] As fate would have it, in January 1306 Bruce was in attendance at the English court, having come south to visit his English estates, when Comyn's message reached Edward, with the promise of documentary evidence to follow.

While waiting for the written proof to arrive, Edward let slip to some of his courtiers that he meant to have the Earl of Carrick arrested the next day and tried for treason. Among those present was the Earl of Gloucester, who was well-disposed towards Bruce. He determined to warn his friend, and sent a servant to Bruce with a gift of twelve silver pennies and a pair of spurs.[6] The hint was taken, and that same night he fled to Scotland accompanied only by two companions. The story goes that nearing the Scottish border they encountered a lone rider heading south who aroused their suspicion. He was discovered to be a messanger from Comyn to Edward, and on examination was found to bear a letter and documents containing proof of Bruce's involvement in the plot, evidence which would surely have condemned Bruce had it reached its intended destination.[7]

After seven days' hard riding – a prodigious effort in winter conditions – Bruce and his companions reached his ancestral stronghold of Lochmaben Castle, to confer with his family and allies as to the next move. The time for dissembling was over, and now was the time for action.

High on the list of priorities was Comyn, who would have to be dealt with, either accommodated or eliminated, if Bruce was to succeed in his bid for the throne. As it transpired, King Edward's justices were holding one of their regular sessions in Dumfries at that time, and it was normal for the great magnates of the land to be at hand on such occasions. As a result John Comyn was in residence at his nearby castle of Dalswinton, and a meeting was arranged between the two great rivals, on neutral ground in Greyfriars Kirk in Dumfries, each to be accompanied by only a small retinue.

Details of what transpired are hazy, with the two men conferring in private before the high altar in the church. What is known is that voices were raised, daggers drawn and blows struck, before Bruce returned to his men exclaiming "I doubt I have slain Comyn!", to which one of his retainers, Roger de Kirkpatrick replied "You doubt? I'll mak siccar!" (I'll make sure), before running into the church to finish the job.[8]

Now the die was cast indeed, and in killing one enemy Bruce created many more. Comyn had powerful friends and allies, and was connected to many of the great families of Scotland with whom Bruce was now engaged in a blood feud, and if he was to gain the crown, he would have to fight half of Scotland as well as Edward of England. If that wasn't a daunting enough prospect, the sacrilege of murder in a church was to earn him excommunication and trouble with the Papacy for years to come. But there could be no turning back. His only hope now of success, indeed survival, was to act, and to act boldly.

Bruce acted boldly indeed. Showing impressive presence of mind in a crisis, Robert immediately rallied his companions and men-at-arms and rode swiftly to Dumfries castle where the justices were in session. The unsuspecting garrison were taken completely by surprise and quickly overpowered, and the constable, Sir Richard Siward, made prisoner. On hearing the fracas outside, the justices barricaded themselves in the great hall of the castle and prepared to defend themselves, but soon surrendered when Bruce offered them the choice of being burned out or a safe conduct over the border.

Robert then repaired to his family's stronghold of Lochmaben and from thence sent urgent letters to mobilise his friends and allies into action, and so effective was their response that it seems likely to have been part of a prearranged plan. In the space of just a few weeks, between them Bruce and his supporters had captured by force or threat the castles of Ayr, Tibbers, and Comyn's own stronghold of Dalswinton. The castle of Rothesay was taken by Bruce's faithful adherent Robert Boyd of Cunningham in a sea-borne assault, and the castle at Dunaverty on Kintyre secured by negotiation.

Together with Dumfries and the Bruce family's own castles such as Lochmaben and Loch Doon, the acquisition of these fortresses gave Robert a significant strategic power-base, effectively taking control of south-west Scotland. He hurried to Glasgow where, confessing his sins before Bishop Wishart, he received absolution for the death of Comyn. It is noteworthy that the Scottish Church steadfastly supported Bruce and the cause of freedom throughout his long struggle, often putting itself at odds with the Papacy in doing so.[9]

It is at this time that one of the protagonists of Byland, indeed one of the great figures of Scottish history, first appears in our story. Bishop Lamberton had in his household a 20-year-old squire, Sir James Douglas, whose father had died in the Tower of London. Lamberton sent the young Douglas to carry a message to Bruce, and according to Barbour -

> *"...he took the road to Lochmaben and near Arickstone he met the Bruce riding with a great company to Scone to be enthroned and made King. And when Douglas saw him coming he rode forward in haste and greeted him and made obeisance very courteously and told him all his conditions*

and who he was and how Clifford held his inheritance. Also that he came to do homage to him as his rightful King and was ready in everything to share his fortune. And when Bruce had heard his desire he received him with much pleasure and gave him men and arms. For he judged that he would be worthy of his fathers who were brave and able men. Thus they made their acquaintance that never afterwards by any chance of any kind was broken while they lived. Their friendship increased ever more and more for Douglas served always loyally and Bruce so wise, strong, and valiant gladly and well rewarded his service."[10]

Bruce then headed north to the Abbey of Scone in Perthshire, where Scottish kings had been enthroned since time immemorial, and on the 25th of March 1306 he was crowned with all due ceremony in the presence of three bishops and four earls. Absent was the Earl of Fife, whose traditional privilege it was to place the crown on the King's head, but the present Earl was a mere youth and held at the English court. So, for the sake of legitimacy and in order that all traditions be observed, the Earl's 19-year-old sister Isabel, Countess of Buchan, had the honour of laying the golden circlet on the head of Robert Bruce, King of Scots.[11]

When news reached Edward that Bruce had seized the throne, his rage was fearsome to behold. He promised the cruellest of deaths for the "crowned traitor", and to anyone who aided him. He appointed his cousin Aymer de Valence, Earl of Pembroke as viceroy over Scotland, with plenary powers to crush the rebellion with the utmost severity, who, after summoning the northern levies, crossed the border at the head of a large army.

Since his coronation King Robert had been gathering forces in the north of the country, and when he heard of Pembroke's approach he advanced to meet him near Perth. When the forces drew close on the 19th of June, Robert issued a challenge under the code of chivalry that the two armies should meet in combat in open ground. Pembroke accepted the challenge but stated that as the hour was late, the contest should take place the following day. Bruce agreed to this proposal, and drew his men a few miles off to rest their horses, cook supper and camp for the night at Methven, a few miles west of Perth. To his lasting shame, Pembroke

Statue of Sir James Douglas, Scottish National Portrait Gallery. (CC licence Stephencdickson)

chose that moment to launch a surprise attack, and the Scots were taken completely unawares as they scrambled for horses, arms and armour. In the resultant melee the Scottish army was completely routed with many slain or captured, the King himself barely escaping in the confusion.[11]

Thus, barely three months after becoming King, his only significant force had been defeated and scattered, with many of his most valiant and loyal adherents killed or captured. In his vindictive rage Edward ordered that all the conventions of chivalry be suspended, and all those taken to be treated as outlaws and hanged, drawn and quartered, or if they were fortunate, beheaded. One exception was the young Thomas Randolph who, due to his friendship with the Earl of Pembroke, was spared and pardoned, on condition he switch sides.

Worse was soon to follow for Bruce in the summer of 1306. By August Pembroke was once again advancing against him and, accompanied by a small force of just 500, he was attempting to reach the Western Isles and the protection of his allies the MacDonalds of Islay. His route forced

Aymer de
Valence, 2nd Earl
of Pembroke.
(© National Library
of Wales)

him into the territory of his sworn enemy John MacDougall of Lorne, son-in-law of the murdered Comyn, where they were ambushed by the clansmen in a narrow pass at Dalrigh near Tyndrum. After some hard fighting Bruce and his party managed to escape, but only after suffering significant loss of men and horses.

Things were now so desperate that Bruce sent his female relatives - his Queen, his daughter Marjory and his sisters Mary and Christina, together with the Countess of Buchan who had placed the crown on his head - to the relative safety of his northern stronghold at Kildrummy, under the protection of his brother Nigel, while he and what remained of his men continued to the West. This security was to prove illusory, as after a short siege Kildrummy Castle was betrayed to the English and the ladies of the court captured while attempting to escape to Orkney.

Once again the English king displayed the depth of his anger and vindictiveness, with Nigel Bruce and the other male captives from Kildrummy being hanged, drawn and quartered at Berwick, and the females imprisoned in extremely harsh conditions.[13]

Two of the women received especially cruel treatment, Isabel Countess of Buchan, and King Robert's sister, Mary Bruce. To his eternal discredit, Edward ordered that both be held in circumstances designed to be particularly grim and humiliating. Each were confined in specially constructed cages which were abutted to the towers of castles and exposed both to public gaze[14] and the elements, Mary at Roxburgh and Isabel at Berwick.[15]

They were allowed no communication with the outside world, their only contact being with the guards who brought them food and water, and the sole concession to their dignity being the convenience of a privy.[16] In the age of chivalry this was a punishment both shocking and unprecedented, and we can only surmise why these two were reserved for such savagery. The Countess of Buchan may well have aroused Edward's resentment for her symbolic role in King Robert's coronation, and it is likely Mary Bruce was marked out because her husband, Sir Neil Campbell, was still actively engaged in arms in the service of her brother. Despite being held in such harsh conditions for four years, the women survived this aspect of their ordeal. In 1310 both were released into milder conditions, Isabel to the custody of the Carmelite nunnery at Berwick, while Mary was moved to Newcastle.

Edward originally planned equal cruelty for Bruce's 12-year-old daughter, the Princess Marjorie. He ordered that a similar cage be prepared in the Tower of London to hold the young girl and instructed that she be allowed no contact with anyone other than Constable of the Tower.[17] However for reasons unknown Edward relented from imposing such barbarity on a child, and instead she was confined in the care of nuns at the Gilbertine Priory of Watton in the East Riding of Yorkshire.

The remaining women prisoners were afforded more lenient but hardly comfortable confinement. Robert's eldest sister Christina Bruce, was held at another Gilbertine establishment, the nunnery of Sixhills in Lincolnshire.[18] It is possible she was spared the fate of her sister Mary because her husband Sir Christopher Seton had recently been hanged, drawn and quartered on Edward's orders at Dumfries, which may have been considered punishment enough.

The last and most important female prisoner was Queen Elizabeth, wife of Robert Bruce. Based on Edward's treatment of the other women, one might have feared the worst on her behalf, but in fact she was confined in less onerous conditions than her fellow captives. Elizabeth was lodged under house arrest in the royal manor house at Burstwick in Holderness, and her relatively mild treatment was surely due to her being the daughter of the Earl of Ulster, one of the King's more powerful and influential supporters. Despite her father's protection, her situation was far from luxurious, being only allowed two ladies-in-waiting who, it was specified, must be 'elderly and not at all gay'.[19] Her status as queen was not recognised, and such was her lack of comfort that it is recorded she complained to Edward that she had 'neither attire for her person or head nor a bed nor furniture for her chamber'.[20]

Queen Elizabeth was to remain a prisoner for eight long years, until freed with Marjorie and Christina and others after Bannockburn in exchange for the Earl of Hereford. Mary Bruce gained her liberty in an earlier exchange in 1312. Sadly the tragic figure of Isabel of Buchan did not survive her captivity. The last reference to her is in 1313 when she was transferred into the custody of Sir Henry Beaumont, who had married her niece, and it can be assumed she died before she could be exchanged with the others in 1314.

While reeling from the death of his brother and the capture of his wife, daughter and sisters, Bruce received another hammer blow. In February 1307 an expedition of 18 ships led by Bruce's younger brothers

Berwick Castle. Isabel Countess of Buchan was held prisoner in a cage suspended from the castle walls, exposed to the elements and public gaze. (© Rosser 1954)

Thomas and Alexander sailed into Loch Ryan in Galloway. The object was to make a landing and move north to link up with another force led by Bruce himself, which would land on the Ayrshire coast. The plans went badly wrong from the beginning, and the party was attacked by a large force as soon as they attempted to land. A few managed to escape, but most were slain or captured, only to be executed later. Both Bruce brothers were badly wounded, but taken alive to Carlisle to be hanged, drawn and quartered on Edward's command, and their heads affixed to spikes above the city gates.

Lesser men would have collapsed under such crushing blows, as described by John of Fordun, a 14th century Scottish chronicler, and there is no exaggeration in his words.

"Great was the task that Robert Bruce took upon himself and unbearable the burdens upon his shoulders. His mishaps, flights and dangers; hardships and weariness; hunger and thirst; watchings and fastings; nakedness and cold; snares and banishment; the seizing, imprisoning, slaughter and downfall of his near ones and – even more – his dear ones, no-one now living, I think, recollects or is equal to rehearsing."[21]

Bruce was to face many years of trial, tribulation, and sacrifice as he strove to retain his tenuous hold on the throne.

Returning from his refuge in the Western Isles, Bruce himself had descended on the Ayrshire coast, in what was intended to be a coordinated operation in tandem with his brothers' ill-fated landing in Galloway. In a night time attempt to surprise Turnberry Castle, he succeeded in killing many of the garrison, and carrying off their horses and a large quantity of supplies, although unable to capture the castle itself.

He now took to the forests and hills of Carrick, taking advantage of the landscape he knew intimately to conduct 'hit and run' operations against the English. As soon as Edward learned that Bruce was back on the mainland he poured huge resources into the hunt for him. He ordered his Scottish allies to mobilise their forces and converge on Carrick, the Macdowalls of Galloway from the south, and MacDougall of Lorne from the north. Aymer de Valence was ordered north from Carlisle leading an army of 3,000, with the objective of trapping their quarry in a tightening noose. To avoid this, Bruce split his already small force into groups of a few men, with orders to disperse, avoid capture, and rendez-vous at predetermined locations.

Throughout the spring of 1307, the Scottish king was a hunted man, often travelling with only one or two companions, and on several occasions only avoiding death or capture through personal courage and his skill with weapons.[22] He was hunted by dogs, and often slept under the stars or in caves, and it was on one such occasion he encountered the apocryphal spider, whose legendary persistence encouraged him to once more attempt when all seemed lost.

Spider or not, he did persist, and gathering his meagre forces, determined to fight on. Those weeks as a hunted fugitive represent the nadir of his career, and slowly, imperceptibly at first, his fortunes began to turn.

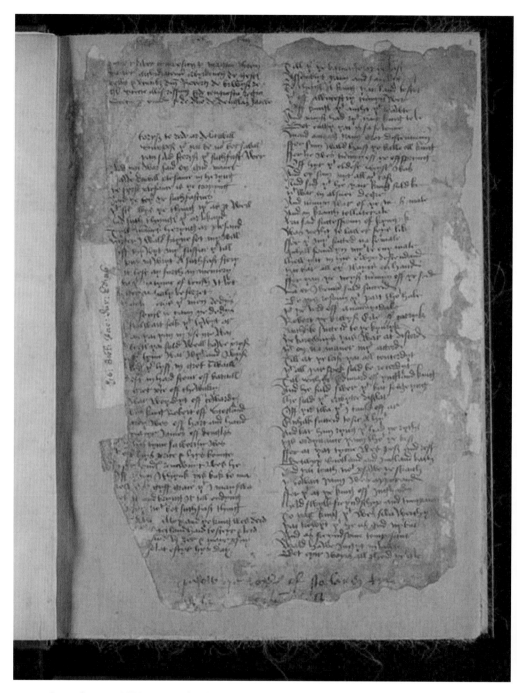

Page from a 1489 copy of 'The Brus' by John Barbour. (© National Library of Scotland)

Edward I spent the last six months of his life at Lanercost Priory before dying at Burgh on Sands in 1307. (Author)

Chapter 6

The Turn of the Tide

The first sign of recovery came in April 1307, when Bruce and several hundred of his men set up camp in an inaccessible part of Glen Trool, deep in the Galloway hills, a spot chosen for its plentiful supply of venison and defensible position. Word reached the Earl of Pembroke of Bruce's location, and taking 1,500 of his best men determined to capture or kill him. The only access to the Scots' camp was by a single path by the lochside, too narrow for the English men-at-arms to deploy and make use of their superior numbers, and instead of taking the Scots unawares, they found them ready and waiting and well-armed. A short, sharp engagement ensued, in which the Scots defended their position, and forced the English to retreat with heavy losses. It was not much more than a skirmish, but the effect on Scottish morale was electrifying. Suddenly they knew they had a leader, a leader who could win, and now men began to flock to his banner.[1]

The Scottish king was now emboldened enough to leave the shelter of the hills and descend to the lowlands of Ayrshire, where he found further recruits to his cause. Aymer de Valence, after retiring briefly to Carlisle to lick his wounds, came north again at the urging of the now-ailing Edward, with a much larger force in the hope of meeting Bruce again, this time in the open field.

On the morning of the 10th of May, Bruce and his army of 600 or so were drawn up in a defensive position at the foot of Loudon Hill, a few miles to the east of the town of Galston. The English army was approaching in full battle-array, and according to the chronicler John Barbour, presented a magnificent sight -

> *"The King saw their squadron coming quite early in the morning, well arrayed in ranks, and behind them, somewhat close at hand, he saw the other following. Their basnets*

were all burnished bright, gleaming in the sun's light; their spears, their pennons and their shields lit up all the fields with light. Their best, bright-embroidered, banners, horse of many hues, coats of armour of diverse colours, and hauberks which were as white as flour, made them glitter as though they were like to angels from the kingdom of Heaven."[2]

Pembroke must have been confident of success – at last he had Bruce where he wanted him, out in the open, and outnumbered four or five to one by English heavy cavalry, but the Scottish king had chosen his ground wisely. He positioned his men at the end of a causeway that ran along the front of the hill, flanked on both sides by marshy ground unsuitable for horses. He then had his men dig a series of deep ditches which served to narrow the approach still further, and limited the width of front they had to defend.

Oblivious to this, Pembroke sounded the charge and his first squadron bore down on the Scots at full speed. Suddenly coming upon the ditches, they swerved inside to avoid them, becoming hopelessly entangled with their comrades who were also being forced in from the other side, before breaking on the Scottish spears in a state of complete confusion. Hundreds were unhorsed and many slain as they reeled back in complete disorder, only to become embroiled with the second squadron as it was caught up in the melee.

Bruce then ordered his men to advance, and the spear-wall moved forward relentlessly, turning the shambles into a rout as the English broke and fled.[3] Pembroke and his shattered force retreated to the safety of Ayr Castle, before returning to Carlisle and resigning his role as Governor of Scotland. This comprehensive victory, together with his recent success at Glen Trool, afforded King Robert a measure of revenge on Aymer de Valence for the damaging defeat that Pembroke had inflicted on him at the Battle of Methven just twelve months previously. The two men were almost exact contemporaries, and would have known each other well from Robert's time at the English court, and their careers had been, and would continue to be, curiously intertwined. Up to this time they had faced each other three times on the battlefield, and in years to come would do so again, firstly at Bannockburn, and again at Byland.

Glen Trool, scene of Bruce's first tentative military success. (J Miall)

King Robert defeated a strong English force under the Earl of Pembroke at Loudon Hill in 1307. (CC A-S 2.0 Iain Thompson)

For months Edward had been lying in his sick-bed at Lanercost Priory near Carlisle, eagerly expecting to hear of the capture of Bruce by one of his commanders. When instead he was told not only of Robert's escape, but also of his subsequent military successes, it was with a mixture of astonishment and rage. Deciding he would have to do the job himself, he resolved to make one final effort to crush the upstart king and his rebellious followers once and for all. The entire feudal power of England was summoned to join him, and casting aside the litter in which he had been carried in for over a year, the aged warrior mounted his horse and once more put himself at the head of his troops. By sheer willpower he drove himself on, but the effort was too great. After travelling only six miles in four days, on the 7th of July 1307 Edward Plantagenet, 'the Hammer of the Scots', died at Burgh-on-Sands, within sight of a still unconquered Scotland.[4]

At a stroke the dynamics of the struggle between the two nations was changed. The crown of England had passed from a determined, capable and ruthless ruler, the foremost soldier of his age, to an indolent, self-indulgent youth with no liking for the rigours of campaign, and little interest in matters of state. The dying king's last request to his son was that his bones should be carried before the invading army until Bruce was beaten and Scotland subjugated. Instead Edward II sent his father's body south for eventual burial in Westminster Abbey, before leading his soldiers on a leisurely perambulation of south-west Scotland, before retiring over the border without striking a blow. The new king would in due course turn his attention to Scotland again, but never with the single-minded and relentless tenacity that so consumed his father.[5]

The Scottish king welcomed this timely and fortuitous deliverance, and used the breathing-space afforded by the easing of English pressure to turn his attention to his Scottish opponents. In so doing, Robert displayed a determination and ruthlessness normally associated with his recently-deceased nemesis, as he dealt with the main English allies in turn. First to feel his wrath were the Macdowalls of Galloway, who had been responsible for the capture and murder of his brothers Alexander and Thomas. In a lightning campaign Galloway was devastated by fire and sword, completely nullifying the Macdowalls as an asset to the English.[6]

It was around this time that Robert's hand was strengthened by the return of his nephew, Thomas Randolph, to his banner. Since his capture

TO COMMEMORATE
THOMAS RANDOLPH
EARL OF MORAY
A DISTINGUISHED SOLD-
IER AND DIPLOMATIST
WHO RECOVERED THIS
CASTLE IN 1313 AFTER
IT HAD BEEN FOR 20
YEARS IN THE HANDS
OF THE ENGLISH

Thomas Randolph, Earl of Moray was King Robert's nephew, and came to be one of his most able and trusted captains. (CC A-S 3.0 David M. Jensen)

at Methven, Randolph had been in the service of Edward I, but he now returned to his uncle's cause (perhaps freed from an oath by Edward's death) and would go on to serve Robert faithfully throughout the long years of struggle. Created Earl of Moray by the King, he proved to be a very capable and inspiring captain, and formed a successful and effective partnership with Sir James Douglas.

Next he struck north, determined to strike at his main enemies, the Comyns, in their own heartland, and in either December 1307 (according to Barbour) or May 1308 (according to Fordun), defeated the Earl of Buchan together with an English contingent at the Battle of Inverurie. The entire province of Buchan was now laid waste from end to end, and visited with such devastation that it would never again serve as a power base against the Scottish crown.[7]

This now left the MacDougalls of Argyll as the strongest remaining English ally, and the last great source of domestic opposition to Bruce.

54

John MacDougall (son of Alexander MacDougall, Lord of Lorne), was a close kinsman of the Comyns, and had ambushed Bruce and his small band in the aftermath of the Battle of Methven some two years previously, killing many of his companions in the process. Now was the time for the reckoning, and Bruce readied his forces to advance into the mountain fastness of Argyll. To reach the MacDougall fortress of Dunstaffnage, the King and his army would have to force the Pass of Brander, a narrow track confined on one side by the waters of Loch Awe, and the steep flank of Ben Cruachan on the other.

Knowing the place to be the perfect location for an ambush, the Lord of Lorne placed a small number of his men to block the path with a barricade, while placing the remainder of his 2,000 men on the mountainside above the track, ready to pounce when the royal army entered the narrow defile. Bruce, however, had been warned by scouts of the enemy dispositions, and sent a strong force of lightly armed highlanders and archers under the command of Sir James Douglas higher up the mountain to out-flank Lorne's men – very similar tactics to those he would employ at the Battle of Byland some fourteen years later.

With a shout the MacDougalls attacked the men-at-arms below them, when at almost the same moment Douglas' men sounded their war-cry and fell upon their unsuspecting foes. Set upon from two sides, the men of Lorne made a brief attempt to stand their ground, but quickly realised their position was hopeless and fled in disorder, suffering many slain and captured.[8] With no organised resistance remaining, the King pressed on to Dunstaffnage Castle, which fell after a short siege. John of Lorne managed to avoid capture, and continued to serve the English cause in years to come, but MacDougall opposition to Bruce was now broken. With the power of his last great domestic rival eliminated, Bruce could now devote his energy to consolidating his control of Scotland, as he and his lieutenants set about clearing the country of the remaining English garrisons.

In the space of a few short years Bruce had gone from a hunted fugitive one step from capture and death, to master of all of Scotland, save a few remaining strongholds in English hands. This remarkable success is due in the main to the abilities and character of the man himself - his courage and tenacity, his skill in arms and tactical expertise, his strategic insight and careful diplomacy – qualities which produced a leader an entire nation could rally to. Although his recovery of fortune had begun

Dunstaffnage Castle was the stronghold of the MacDougalls of Lorne, the most powerful of the English allies in Scotland. This formidable fortress was captured by Bruce after his victory at the Battle of the Pass of Brander in 1308. (CC A-S 3.0 Guillaume Piolle)

before the Death of Edward I, there is no doubt the accession of Edward of Caernarvon to the English throne, and the domestic upheaval which ensued, was greatly fortuitous for Bruce and the Scottish cause.

Edward II was cut from a different cloth than his father, although by all accounts he enjoyed the same advantages of imposing stature, comely appearance and kingly bearing. Sadly for England, the favourable comparisons ended there, as the new king gave way to the self-indulgent and hedonistic side of his nature. He was much more interested in seeking enjoyment than the serious business of statecraft and war, and greatly preferred the company of his relatively low-born favourites to the counsel of the leading men of his court. For much of his reign this was to bring him into conflict with his nobles and barons, particularly his obsession with Piers Gaveston, a Gascon knight and boyhood companion, whom he showered with gifts and elevated to the Earldom of Cornwall, a title previously only given to members of the royal family.[9]

Fuelled by their grievances, a group of nobles and leading clergy headed by the Earls of Lancaster and Warwick, who became known as the Lords Ordainers, banded together to present a set of demands or Ordinances to the King, and their continuing conflicts and disharmony provided a much-needed 'breathing space' for the Scots.

While the English king and his aristocracy were preoccupied with civil discord, King Robert took advantage of their distraction to steadily recover those Scottish castles which remained in English hands. One by one the great strongholds were reduced by starvation, escalade or stratagem, including Banff (1310), Ayr (1311), Dirleton (1311), Perth (1312), Dumfries and Caerlaverock (1313), and Roxburgh and Edinburgh (1314).

From time to time Edward and his barons attempted to patch up their differences in order to deal with the deteriorating situation in Scotland, but with little success. In the autumn of 1309 two large armies were mustered at Carlisle and Berwick, but the campaign was abandoned before it was started. In September of the following year Edward tried again, leading a huge army into Scotland accompanied by Gaveston

Dirleton Castle. This thirteenth-century stronghold of the de Vaux family was captured by the English in 1298 and recaptured by Bruce's forces in 1311. (Author)

and the Earls of Gloucester and Surrey. Employing a tactic he was to use effectively on a number of occasions, King Robert refused to give battle to the greater force, and simply fell back before the invading host, wasting the land and driving off livestock as he retreated. Completely baffled and frustrated by the Scots' tactics, Edward's army wandered throughout southern Scotland before want of provisions forced them back over the border by the end of October.[10]

The initiative had now passed firmly to the Scots, and in 1311 Bruce led two great raids into the border counties of England, pillaging and extorting tribute from the defenceless inhabitants. The Lanercost chronicler describes them in almost prosaic fashion -

> *"...having collected a great army, he* (King Robert) *entered England at Solway on the Thursday before the feast of Assumption;* (12th August) *and he burned all the land of the lord of Gilsland and the vill of Haltwhistle and a great part of Tynedale, and after eight days he returned to Scotland, taking with him a great booty of animals; nevertheless he had killed few men apart from those who wished to defend themselves by resistance."*

and barely a month later -

> *"About the feast of the Nativity of the Blessed Virgin* (8th September), *Robert returned with an army into England, directing his march towards Northumberland, and passing by Harbottle and Holystone and Redesdale, he burnt the district around Corbridge, destroying everything; also he caused more men to be killed than on the former occasion. And so he turned into the valleys of North and South Tyne, laying waste those parts which he had previously spared, and returned into Scotland after 15 days; nor could the wardens whom the King of England had stationed on the marches oppose so great a force of Scots as he brought with him."*[11]

The conflict between Edward and the Lords Ordainers had broken out into a civil war which swung one way then the other. In May 1312 Gaveston sought refuge in Scarborough Castle while Edward was elsewhere

Edward II, a drawing of the effigy on his tomb in Gloucester Cathedral. (© British Library)

seeking to raise troops. After a short siege he surrendered himself into the custody of the Earl of Pembroke on condition that his life be spared. But as he was being transported south, he was seized by forces loyal to the Earls of Warwick and Lancaster, and after a brief trial, executed on the 19th of June.

Edward's reaction to the death of his favourite was one of grief and rage; however, circumstances prevented him from seeking immediate retribution, and King Robert determined to take full advantage of the domestic English discord by launching a large-scale invasion of Westmorland, Northumberland, and deep into County Durham.

> *"When Robert Bruce heard of this discord in the south, having assembled a great army, he invaded England about the feast of the Assumption of the Blessed Virgin* (15th August) *and burned the towns of Hexham and Corbridge and the western parts, and took booty and much spoil and prisoners, nor was there anyone who dared to resist. While he halted in peace and safety near Corbridge he sent part of his army as far as Durham, which, arriving there suddenly on market day, carried off all that was found in the town, and gave a great part of it to the flames, cruelly killing all who opposed them, but scarcely attacking the castle and priory."*[12]

Such was the shock and terror of these depredations, that the traumatised burghers of Durham agreed to purchase a truce until midsummer of 1313, for the enormous sum of £2,000 (the equivalent of well over £1,000,000 today) followed quickly by their northern neighbours in Northumberland who, fearing they might suffer a similar fate, reached an accommodation with the Scots on the same terms.[13]

Meanwhile, emissaries from Pope Clement V had arrived in England in response to a plea from Edward, including the Queen's uncle Prince Louis of Évreux, and they had been busy striving to bring the two warring factions together, with some success. In October 1313 an agreement was reached in which the Ordainers, in return for a full admission of their guilt in the death of Gaveston, received Edward's pardon.[14]

Such an accommodation, where previously they could find no common ground, had seemed highly unlikely just a few months earlier amidst the bitterness surrounding Gaveston's judicial murder. But grave news from Scotland provided the catalyst that made a settlement possible, indeed necessary.

As a contemporary chronicler puts it - *"...for the capture of his castles Edward could scarcely restrain his tears. He summoned the earls and barons to come to his aid and overcome the traitor who calls himself king."*[15]

Only a handful of castles remained in English hands north of the border, one of them being Stirling, one of the strongest and certainly the most important strategically in the entire kingdom. It had been invested by a Scottish army under Edward Bruce, the king's brother, who had

Durham Cathedral. On no fewer than six occasions between 1312 and 1327 Durham paid heavily to obtain truces from the Scots. (CC A-S 2.0 G Campbell Hall)

come to an arrangement with the Governor of the castle, Sir Thomas Mowbray, that unless Stirling was relieved by an English army by Midsummer's Day 1314, it would be surrendered to the Scots.[16]

The prospect of the most important fortress in the land falling to the Scots, and the fatal blow to English interests in Scotland that would represent, to say nothing of the national humiliation that would ensue, was enough for Edward and the Lords Ordainer to set aside their factional aims for the common good.

King Robert was aghast when he heard of the arrangement his brother had entered into, which in an instant undid his careful policy of many years to avoid meeting a superior English army in the field. Now, in order to uphold his brother's honour, he would have to risk all in the hazard of battle in order to prevent the relief of Stirling Castle. For Edward the opposite was true – at last he had his opponent where he wanted him, obliged to meet in a pitched battle where the full might of England could be brought to bear, in which he would have every advantage.

For once Edward displayed some of his father's energy and enthusiasm for war, as he prepared for his campaign in the summer of 1314. Summons were issued to eight earls and their retainers to bring their feudal levies to Berwick by the 10th of June. Supplemented by troops from Ireland and archers and spearmen from Wales, it was to be the largest army ever assembled by a medieval king of England for a foreign expedition. The army which advanced into Scotland on the 17th of June consisted of 2,500 mounted knights, 3,000 archers, and 15,000 infantry, a massive host by the standards of the day.[17]

By comparison the Scottish army which would try to oppose them was piteously small, consisting of 5 - 6,000 spearmen, a few hundred archers, and about 500 light horse. In their favour was the fact that they were disciplined and well-trained, fighting on their own ground, and superbly led by a skilled and inspirational leader.[18]

As the massive English army approached Stirling on the 23rd of June, King Robert picked his ground carefully in order to give his heavily-outnumbered force a fighting chance. Choosing a strong defensive position near a stream called the Bannockburn, he manoeuvred his opponents onto ground unsuitable for heavy cavalry, and into a position where their superior numbers could not be brought into play. In a hard-fought battle over two days, the English army was first repulsed, then completely routed with great slaughter. King Edward himself narrowly

The Battle of Bannockburn, as depicted in the Holkham Bible of 1327-35. (© British Library)

escaped capture, taking flight in a fishing boat from Dunbar, but many of his great retainers were not so lucky, and it is said Scotland grew rich on the booty taken and ransoms received. Among those taken was the Earl of Hereford, whose freedom was only purchased by Edward through the return of Bruce's Queen, Elizabeth, his daughter and sister, and several other high-ranking prisoners. Stirling Castle was duly surrendered under the terms of the agreement, and the few remaining English garrisons in Scotland soon followed suit, with the sole exception of Berwick.

(The story of the Battle of Bannockburn cannot be told here, but is well worthy of further reading and study in its own right.)[19]

At Bannockburn the Scots had triumphed in one of the great set-piece battles of medieval history, and after eighteen years of warfare, invasion and occupation, Scotland was finally free of English control. But, as events were to prove, although King Robert had prevailed on the battlefield, the war was yet to be won, and Scotland had not seen the last of Edward of Caernarfon.

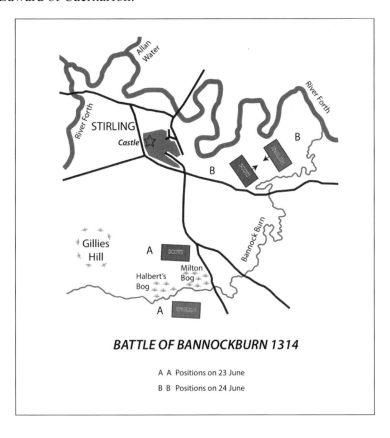

BATTLE OF BANNOCKBURN 1314

A A Positions on 23 June

B B Positions on 24 June

Heavily fortified castles offered some protection from the Scottish raiders. The people of Bamburgh were said to fold up their wooden houses and carry them into the castle. (Amy Clelland)

Chapter 7

1314 to 1322 – Border Warfare

"After the aforesaid victory, Robert the Bruce was commonly called King of Scotland by all men, because he had acquired Scotland by force of arms."[1]

Thus wrote an English chronicler in the aftermath of Bannockburn. Despite the scale and the humiliating circumstances of his defeat, or perhaps because of them, King Edward was still unwilling to accept the legitimacy of Bruce's kingship. Notwithstanding their great victory, the Scots had no desire to prolong the war, and offered peace for the simple price of recognition of Scottish independence and Robert's right to the throne.

As a conciliatory gesture, King Robert returned to the English king, unasked and without condition, the Great Seal of England and the Royal Shield, both of which had been lost at Bannockburn. But Edward's proud and obstinate character caused him to reject all overtures of peace. It became obvious to Bruce therefore, that the only way to bring Edward to terms was to make continuation of the fighting so costly for the English that it would force him to negotiate a peace, so the decision was made to carry the war across the border into England with even greater intensity.

Accordingly, in August 1314 a Scottish force under Edward Bruce and Sir James Douglas raided into Northumberland and Durham, penetrating as far south as Richmond in Yorkshire, pillaging and carrying off plunder as they went, before returning via Cumberland. Later in the same year a column under Bruce himself harried the Tyne valley, demanding homage and exacting tribute in silver, goods and cattle.

This pattern of warfare was to afflict the northern counties of England on a continual basis for the next decade and beyond. Widespread depredations by the Scots became an annual event, with sometimes two or even three raids taking place in the same year. What little opposition that could be mustered was half-hearted and disorganised, and many communities, abandoned by their king and feudal overlords, took the pragmatic decision that compliance was better than resistance. Such was the extent of Scottish ascendancy over the border counties that they became, in effect, part of the Kingdom of Scotland, in terms of of taxation and revenue.

Unfortunately for the people of the North of England, their sufferings seemed peripheral and far removed from the peaceful and secure Midlands and South, where the King and his great magnates held most of their land and wealth. Almost immediately after the Bannockburn campaign, Edward renewed his struggle with his troublesome nobles, led by his rebellious cousin, Thomas Earl of Lancaster, with the ensuing civil discord so preoccupying both parties that Scottish affairs were neglected for years on end.[2]

Meanwhile the Scots, after a setback in 1315 when a concerted attempt to capture Carlisle Castle ended in failure, sought to maintain the

Easby Abbey near Richmond suffered from frequent Scottish raids. Ironically the greatest damage it suffered was when English soldiers were billeted there prior to the Battle of Neville's Cross in 1346. (Author)

An ancient manuscript date c. 1322. It shows two warriors, possibly St. George and the Earl of Lancaster, with typical arms and armour of the period. (© Bodleian Library)

military pressure on a number of fronts. In midsummer 1316 the King himself led a large force into England, reaching into Yorkshire, where he was only dissuaded from burning Richmond by a large sum of money, then turning west he ravaged the country as far as Furness in Lancashire, before returning unmolested over the border, rich with booty.

For the remainder of that year and throughout 1317, the north enjoyed a temporary respite from such damaging incursions, as the attention of the Scots was temporarily diverted elsewhere. King Robert, seeing Edward's apparent apathy towards to the suffering of his northern subjects, had determined to find out if the English king would be equally indifferent to an attack on his Irish possessions. A strong Scottish army landed in Ireland in 1315 under Edward Bruce, and gained some success in a series of victories over Anglo-Irish forces. They were joined in the autumn of 1316 by King Robert with further reinforcements, but despite winning a hard-fought battle against the Earl of Ulster near Dublin, had been unable to capture the city. The rest of the campaign

Carlisle Castle withstood several determined attempts by the Scots to capture it. However, it was unable to prevent repeated Scottish incursions into England. (Author)

was unsatisfactory, being dogged by famine, plague, and unreliable Irish allies, and the King returned to Scotland at the end of May 1317.[3]

On hearing that Bruce was in Ireland, Edward and his nobles once again attempted to set aside their differences in order to launch an invasion of Scotland, and each side agreed to bring their forces to Newcastle in October 1316. However, such was the level of rivalry and mistrust between them, that the enterprise fell apart before it could begin and the opportunity to take advantage of King Robert's absence was lost.[4]

After his disappointment in Ireland, the Scottish king set his sights on a greater prize. Since its capture and sack at the hands of Edward I twenty-two years previously, Berwick had remained firmly in English hands. Edward had replaced the previous wooden palisade with a strong stone wall and ditch 80 feet wide and 40 feet deep – defences which had comfortably withstood previous Scottish attacks. It was the last remaining English garrison in Scotland, and as such it was vital, not only strategically as the 'springboard' to Scotland, but for the maintenance of English prestige.

Bruce gathered his army in secret at various locations near Berwick, and began to construct siege engines. In the end they were not needed, as a Scottish sympathiser in charge of guarding a section of the city

The Charter of Carlisle of 1316. The illustration depicts an unsuccessful Scottish siege. The knight in the plumed helmet is Sir Andrew de Harcla. (© Cumbria Archives)

Richmond Castle provided a welcome refuge for many local people from the depredations of the Scots. (Author)

wall allowed a scaling party led by Douglas and Moray to breach the defences unopposed, and hold it long enough for Robert and his main army to arrive and take possession of the town. The castle garrison held out for a further few weeks before being starved into submission, thus clearing Scotland of English soldiers for the first time since 1296.[5]

Elated by this success, King Robert did not rest on his laurels, instead he launched an invasion which ventured further into England than any of his previous incursions. The castles of Wark, Harbottle and Mitford were captured, before taking fire and sword into the heart of Yorkshire. Northallerton and Boroughbridge were burned, and in Knaresborough only 20 houses out of 160 were spared the flames.[6] Ripon escaped a similar fate only by paying an enormous ransom of a thousand marks,[7] before the Scots returned north of the border, driving *'a countless quantity of cattle before them, carrying them off to Scotland without any opposition.'*[8]

Right: Knaresborough Castle held out against the Scots, but could not prevent them burning most of the town in 1318. Using Knaresborough as a base, they raided into lower Wharfedale, pillaging Wetherby and Tadcaster. (Author)

Below: Ripon Cathedral. The townspeople sought refuge in the cathedral when the Scots arrived in 1318. After negotiations, the town was spared on the promise of 1,000 marks, with six prominent citizens taken as hostage. (Author)

In the two years since their aborted invasion plan, relations between the King and his disaffected nobility had deteriorated steadily to the verge of civil war. Now, thanks to the diplomatic efforts of the Earl of Pembroke, a precarious truce had been brokered which saw both parties set aside their grievances in order to make a united response to the crisis in the north. The loss of Berwick was an affront to national pride, and the damaging incursions by the Scots deep into England could not go unanswered.

In June 1319 the joint forces of King Edward and his nobles assembled at Newcastle, with the aim of recovering Berwick and, if possible, to bring the Scots' army to battle and destroy it. Estimated at some 12,000 men, it was not as great as the vast army that had followed Edward north of the border in 1314, but still more than twice as many as the Scots could put in the field. The army was supported by a fleet of over 70 ships, which would beset the walls from the seaward side, and ensure Berwick could not be relieved by sea. When all preparations had been made, the great army moved north, and by the first week in September had completely surrounded the town on the landward side, and enforced a blockade from the sea.

On its recovery from the English, King Robert had placed the defence of Berwick in the hands of his son-in-law Sir Walter the Steward (Walter Stewart), and for the past year he had been assiduously preparing for

the inevitable English attempt to recapture it. The defences had been heightened and strengthened, and the garrison well stocked with provisions, and manned with well-armed and disciplined soldiers.

On the 7th of September a coordinated attack from land and sea was launched on all sides, but after a day of hard fighting the defenders held firm. The attackers then spent some days constructing various large siege engines with which to assault the walls, and these

Arms of Walter the Steward.

were brought to bear in the next great onslaught which took place on the 13th. To meet this challenge, the defenders brought up a large catapult, which succeeded in disabling the siege engines with huge boulders, then setting them on fire. Once again the Scots held out, but with heavy casualties on both sides, the numbers defending the walls was growing thin in some sections.[9]

All the while Bruce was nearby watching events carefully. He knew the defenders could not hold out indefinitely, but was reluctant to challenge a superior force in an attempted relief. Instead he set in motion a bold plan to force the English to abandon the siege.

When Edward moved north to join Lancaster at Newcastle, he left his Queen Isabella to await his return in comfortable lodgings near York. All of the English forces in the north of England lay before the walls of Berwick, leaving everything between the Scottish border and the Humber unprotected. King Robert conceived of a plan to send a strong yet fast and mobile force to York with the aim of capturing Isabella, thereby not only raising the siege of Berwick, but bringing the entire war to an end by forcing Edward to make peace. It was a bold plan, and one which almost worked.

So it was by the 11[h] of September, a strong Scottish force under the command of the Earl of Moray and Sir James Douglas lay at Myton, near Boroughbridge, at the point where the Swale meets the Ouse, some 12 miles north of York, awaiting contact from agents in the city.

Bruce was being kept informed of Isabella's situation by his spies in the city of York, but by ill-luck one of these was discovered, and under threat of torture he revealed the plan to the city authorities. When this was first reported to Archbishop William Melton of York he was at first incredulous, but when scouts confirmed that a Scottish army was indeed where the spy said it would be, he promptly sent Isabella by boat out of harm's way to Nottingham, and set about marshalling his forces.

Unfortunately for the Archbishop, just three days earlier King Edward had ordered the entire York Militia to march north to join the siege of Berwick, so the only men available to confront the Scots were drawn from the citizens of York, yeomen from the surrounding countryside, priests, clerics, and various other clergymen. Nonetheless he was able to muster a substantial force, perhaps around 10,000 men, which was led by the Archbishop himself, together with the Bishop of Ely and Nicholas Fleming, the Mayor of York. This number was probably

The Earl of Moray and Sir James Douglas were King Robert's most trusted captains, and forged a formidable partnership over many years of constant warfare. Their devastating victory at Myton forced Edward II to break off his siege of Berwick. (Chris Rock)

around twice that of their opponents, but the Scottish army consisted of experienced, disciplined and battle-hardened soldiers, led by two of the ablest commanders of the day.

Archbishop Melton perhaps dreamed of emulating his illustrious predecessor Thurstan, who led an army to defeat David I of Scotland at Northallerton in 1138, but when the two forces met on the 12th of September the result was a crushing defeat for the English, with a great many slain in the battle, or drowning in a desperate attempt to escape across the Swale. Among the thousands who perished was the Mayor of York, and the slaughter only came to an end through the onset of darkness.[10,11]

News of the disaster reached the English camp at Berwick on the 14th of September, and Edward immediately took counsel among his leading men as to what action to take. Opinion was divided. The southern lords wanted to continue with the siege, claiming that one final push was all

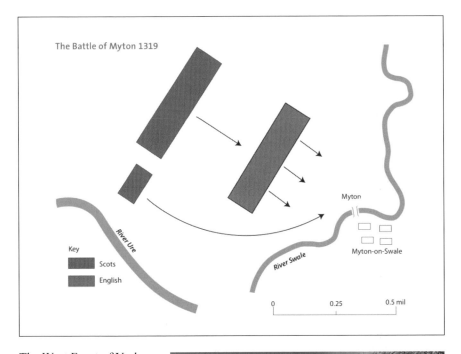

The West Front of York Minster. The image of Archbishop Melton still looks down from his alcove above the Great West Door, despite his crushing defeat at Myton in 1319. (Author)

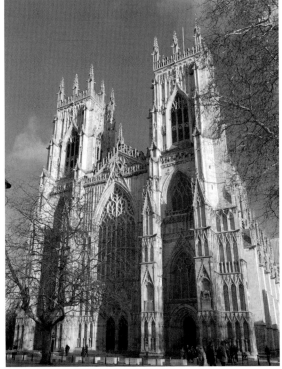

that was required for victory. The northern lords, headed by the Earl of Lancaster, insisted that the siege must be abandoned in order that their men could return to defend their estates against the Scots invaders. When the King inclined to the former, Lancaster and his followers unilaterally withdrew their forces from the siege and headed south, depriving a bitterly disappointed Edward of a third of his army, and leaving him with no option but to call off the siege.

Surprisingly perhaps, Moray and Douglas did not follow up their success with an attack on York itself, choosing instead to plunder softer targets throughout Yorkshire, reaching as far south as the River Aire at Castleford. The aim seems to have been to spread devastation as widely as possible, with eighty-four towns and villages recorded as having suffered destruction at the hands of the raiders. After ransacking large parts of Yorkshire, the Scots turned west via Wharfdale and, after visiting similar devastation on parts of Lancashire, returned to Scotland by way of Westmoreland and Cumberland, laden with booty and hostages after three weeks in England.[12]

Meanwhile Edward delayed in Northumberland with the remainder of his still considerable army, in the rather ingenuous hope of cutting off Moray and Douglas on their return journey to Scotland. When he heard that the Scots had withdrawn via the western marches, he lingered in the north for some weeks, before disbanding his army towards the end of October.

King Robert was relentless in maintaining pressure, and no sooner had the English forces been demobilised, when he ordered Douglas to lead a further devastating incursion into Westmorland and Cumberland on the 1st of November. Unable to mount any meaningful defence, and with his barons in a state of near-rebellion, Edward was forced to negotiate for a truce. This was agreed by King Robert, and it was agreed that it would last for two years from 1st January 1320.[13]

The truce was to provide the northern counties much-needed relief from the depredations of the raiders, but the temporary lifting of the Scottish threat merely served to unleash the forces of civil discord throughout England, as the simmering discontent among the nobility boiled over into open insurrection.

The cause of this was, as ever, Edward's ability to choose favourites who aroused particular jealousy and resentment among the great lords. Hugh Despenser the younger had now assumed the position previously

Above: The late 13th and early 14th centuries saw York's city defences strengthened with stone walls and numerous towers, in face of the Scottish threat. (Author)

Below: Clifford's Tower is almost all that remains of York's medieval castle. The administrative offices of state were moved from Westminster to York on several occasions during the Scottish wars, in 1319-20, in 1322-23, and again in 1327. (Author)

Late 13th C. depiction of a battle scene, illustrating arms and armour of the period.
(© Cambridge University Library)

held by Piers Gaveston before his violent death at the hands of the Earl of Lancaster and his allies. Despenser, together with his namesake father, angered the Marcher Lords by their attempts (with Edward's tacit approval) to grab land and influence in Wales, and this led directly to open rebellion, with the Marcher Lords, encouraged and supported by Lancaster, moving in force upon London. Edward was intimidated enough to send the Despensers into exile, and for a while it seemed the rebellious earls held the upper hand. However their tenuous alliance soon began to fracture, and Edward, for once acting decisively and boldly, seized the opportunity to regain the initiative within 6 months. The Despensers were recalled from exile, and moving quickly against the Marcher Lords, the King either forced their surrender or defeated them in turn. Growing in confidence Edward headed north to deal with Lancaster, who he regarded as the source of the majority of his problems, once and for all.[14]

Lancaster had been joined by the Earl of Hereford who had fled as Edward advanced against him, and together they posted their army at Burton-on-Trent to dispute the King's passage of the river. Edward, however, cleverly turned this position by fording the Trent upstream and forced the rebels to retire before the royal army to Lancaster's main stronghold of Pontefract Castle.

Dunstanburgh Castle, built by Thomas, Earl of Lancaster as a symbol of his power. It is uncertain if it was intended as a bulwark against the Scots, or as a demonstration of his opposition to Edward II. (Author)

The rebel lords were then forced to retreat further northwards, heading towards Lancaster's great castle at Dunstanburgh on the Northumberland coast, and hoping to link up with the Scots, who had once again entered the north of England in force after the expiry of the truce on 1st January 1322.

On reaching Boroughbridge on the 15th of March Lancaster found that Andrew Harclay, the governor of Carlisle, already summoned by Edward and marching south to join the royal army, had heard of the rebels' whereabouts and had arrived before him with a strong force. Harclay had seized both the bridge and ford, the only two points where an army could cross the Ure. The next day the rebels tried to force the crossing but were repulsed with heavy losses, including Hereford who was killed trying to take the bridge. Trapped between Harclay and a detachment of the main royal army under the Sheriff of York approaching from the south, and with his remaining men melting away through desertion, Lancaster surrendered. He was brought before the King at his own former castle of Pontefract, and after a perfunctory 'trial' was decapitated, only his noble rank and royal blood sparing him the full punishment for treason of being hanged, drawn and quartered.[15]

The execution of Thomas, 2nd Earl of Lancaster. Only his royal blood spared him from the more ignominious traitor's death. (The Luttrell Psalter © British Library)

Rievaulx Abbey. King Edward's headquarters before the battle, and scene of his near-capture by Walter the Steward. (Author)

Chapter 8

The Road to Byland

After the Battle of Boroughbridge in March 1322, Edward found himself at the apogee of his reign. Finally freed from the constraints of troublesome barons, he now determined to deal once and for all with the Scots, and he wrote confidently to the Pope that he was *'determined to establish peace by force of arms'*.[1] A compliant Parliament held at York agreed to finance his plans, and every village in England was ordered to provide a fully-armed foot soldier, to supplement the heavy cavalry supplied by the feudal levies. Additional forces of archers, and crossbowmen were summoned from Wales and as far away as Aquitaine, to create a huge host of some 20 to 25 thousand men, even greater than that which had come to grief at Bannockburn.[2]

King Robert refused to be over-awed by such a vast army and instead put into action his well-rehearsed plans to counter the threat. Even as the English army was mustering, he launched a devastating raid through the West Marches, following the coast deep into England as far as Lancaster, which was burned to the ground. There he was joined by another party under Moray and Douglas which had arrived by another route, and together they continued south to Preston, eighty miles from the border, which was also put to the torch. The Chronicler of Lanercost was well placed to record the detail...

> *"Robert de Brus invaded England with an army by way of Carlisle in the week before the Nativity of St. John the Baptist (17th June), and burnt the bishop's manor at Rose, and Allerdale, and plundered the monastery of Holm Cultram, not withstanding that his father's body was buried there; and thence proceeded to lay waste and plunder Copeland, and so on beyond the sands of Duddon to Furness. But the Abbot of Furness...paid ransom for the district... Also they went*

*further beyond the sands of Leven to Cartmel, and burnt the
lands round the priory...and so they crossed the sands of Kent
as far as the town of Lancaster, which they burnt..."*[3]

Withdrawing north again they spent five days trampling crops around
Carlisle, before recrossing the border after three weeks in England,
laden with booty.

But even a devastating raid on that scale could not prevent the English
invasion from taking place, so Robert ordered the implementation of the
next phase of his strategy - that all of south-east Scotland be subject to
'scorched earth' tactics. The entire population was ordered to evacuate,
and with all livestock driven off, all crops carried away and anything
that could not be removed despoiled, every dwelling destroyed and even
the wells poisoned; there was nothing that the vast invading army could
live on apart from what it could carry.

Edward crossed the border at the beginning of August and, ignoring
the Scottish garrison at Berwick, marched through the barren and wasted

The portcullis at Carlisle
Castle. (Author)

landscape unopposed, but watched every step of the way by Sir James Douglas and his scouts. The huge size of Edward's army was also its greatest weakness, as it presented an enormous logistical challenge to keep adequately supplied. The formations had been instructed to bring provisions sufficient for 16 days, but progress had been so slow that these supplies had largely been exhausted by the time the army crossed the border. A combination of contrary winds and harrying by Scottish privateers and their Flemish allies prevented the English supply ships reaching the now starving army, which by the 19th of August had reached the port of Leith, just outside Edinburgh.[4]

Any small groups of soldiers who left the main body to forage for food were mercilessly picked off by Douglas and his fast-moving troopers, as were any stragglers who fell behind, so the English were forced to send out large formations on foraging expeditions, seeking safety in numbers. However, there was nothing to be found, apart from when one lame cow was found near Tranent, which according to Barbour caused the Earl of Surrey to exclaim -

> *"This is the dearest beef I ever saw; for a fact, it cost a thousand pounds and more."*[5]

The lack of food, combined with the Fabian tactics of the Scots, soon compelled a frustrated Edward to order the retreat, and dysentery and other disease afflicted the disintegrating host as it struggled to the border. The Lanercost Chronicle described it thus -

> *'The Scots retired before him in their usual way, nor dared to give him battle. Thus the English were compelled to evacuate Scottish ground before 8 September owing as much to provender as to pestilence in the army; for famine killed as many soldiers as did dysentery.'*[6]

The starving army had been close to mutiny as it waited in vain for the supply ships at Edinburgh, and now as it retreated south, order and discipline began to break down completely. Growing desperate in their search for food, English soldiers took to despoiling religious establishments normally regarded as sacrosanct, as described by the chronicler John of Fordun -

Right: King Alexander III as a guest of Edward I at an English Parliament. (© The Royal Collection)

Below: The magnificent equestrian statue of King Robert the Bruce at Bannockburn. Unveiled by Her Majesty Queen Elizabeth in 1964, on the anniversary of her ancestor's great victory. (Author)

Contemporary image of Edward I – Westminster Abbey Sedilia.
(© Dean and Chapter of Westminster Abbey)

Edward II being offered a crown, possibly that of Scotland.
(© British Library)

Above: Rievaulx Abbey. King Edward's headquarters before the battle, and scene of his near-capture by Walter the Steward. (Author)

Below: Byland Abbey. It is likely King Edward was based here during the battle, before retreating back to Rievaulx Abbey. (Author)

Above: Looking north-west from the top of Sutton Bank. This view shows the Scots' line of march as they approached from Northallerton. They would have deployed south of Gormire Lake before the attack up the narrow and precipitous pass. (Author)

Below: Roulston Scar and Hood Hill, looking south from Sutton Bank. This view shows the route the Scots took around the base of the escarpment to flank the English position. (Author)

Above: Sutton Bank. A view of the A170 as it snakes up the escarpment. Even with its switchbacks the modern road has a gradient of 1 in 4: the medieval track would have been much steeper. (Author)

Below: The view looking north at Whitestone Cliff shows the precipitous nature of the escarpment, and illustrates why the Scots had to force the pass at Sutton Bank. (Author)

Above: Artist's impression of the Battle of Byland. This imagining depicts the climax of the fight at Sutton Bank, as the Scots force their way to the summit in the face of fierce resistance. Four of the main protagonists can be identified from their livery - left to right, Sir Thomas Ughtred, Thomas Randolph Earl of Moray, Sir James Douglas, and Sir Ralph Cobham. (Chris Rock)

Below: Aerial view of Sutton Bank. The Scottish army would have deployed to the south of Gormire Lake (in the lower left of the photograph), while the English assumed a strong defensive position in the narrow pass, roughly where the A170 cuts through the trees in this image, and along the crest of the escarpment shown by the modern footpath. (Kimberli Werner)

Above: A depiction from the fourteenth-century Maciejowski Bible showing medieval warfare and contemporary arms and armour, with a king carrying off captives and pillaged livestock. A scene repeated frequently in the northern counties of England during this period. (© The Morgan Library, New York)

Right: A horse harness pendant emblazoned with the arms of Edward II, found at Rievaulx Abbey, believed lost in his hurried flight from the Scottish army in the wake of the battle. The original artefact can be viewed in the museum at Rievaulx Abbey. (© Historic England Archives)

A fourteenth-century house being pillaged – the fate of many properties at the hands of the Scots in the North of England at this time. (© British Library)

ALE RANDOLPH JAMES ROBT BRUCE WALLACE
DAVID MORAY DOUG- CTESS BUCHAN
II -LAS

Above: Scene from a mural showing the *'Dramatis Personae'* of the Scottish War of Independence. (© Scottish National Portrait Gallery)

Left: A Memorial Stone erected to commemorate the 700th anniversary of the Battle of Byland on the 14th of October 2022, unveiled jointly by the author and the Honourable Adam Bruce, son of the Earl of Elgin and direct descendant of King Robert. (Author)

'...having first sacked and plundered the monasteries of Holyrood in Edinburgh, and of Melrose, and brought them to great desolation. For, in the said monastery of Melrose, on his way back from Edinburgh, the lord William of Peebles, prior of that same monastery, one monk who was then sick, and two lay-brethren, were killed in the dormitory by the English, and a great many monks were wounded unto death. The Lord's Body was cast forth upon the high altar, and the pyx wherein it was kept was taken away. The monastery of Dryburgh was utterly consumed with fire, and reduced to dust; and a great many other holy places did the fiery flames consume, at the hands of the aforesaid king's (Edward II) forces. But God rewarded them therefore, and it brought them no good.'[7]

It brought them no good indeed. According to Barbour, a force commanded by Sir James Douglas came upon the 300-strong English advance party as they were in the act of pillaging Melrose Abbey, killing all but a few of them. This was the fate of many of the retreating army who were harassed at every turn by the Scottish horsemen who mercilessly slaughtered anyone leaving the main force to forage for supplies in the hostile territory.[8]

By early September King Edward re-entered England, his grandiose plans for the final conquest of Scotland in ruins, and with his great army, decimated by famine and disease, straggling behind him.

Forever strategically aware, King Robert now saw the opportunity that presented itself to take advantage of Edward's deteriorated military position. He quickly responded to the English retreat by mobilising the Scottish army, which had been withdrawn safely out of harm's way beyond the Firth of Forth, and swiftly marching across country to invade England through the West Marches. On either the 30th of September or the 1st of October he crossed the Solway at Bowness to begin his campaign that was to culminate at Byland three weeks later.

In the north the main bulwark against the Scots was the garrison at Carlisle Castle maintained by the Governor, Andrew Harclay, recently created Earl of Carlisle for his services to King Edward at Boroughbridge. This company consisted of 280 mounted men-at-arms, together with 500 hobelars (irregular light cavalry), a strong force which

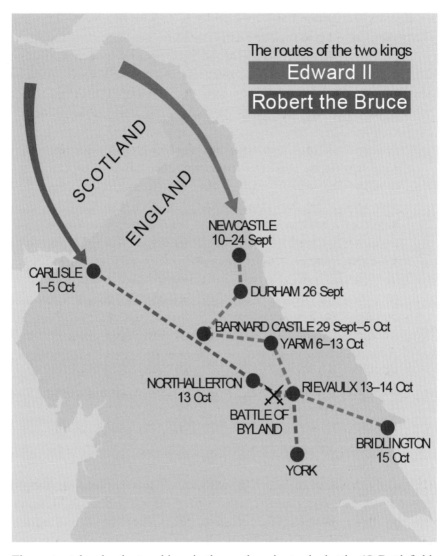

The routes of the two kings

Edward II

Robert the Bruce

SCOTLAND

ENGLAND

CARLISLE
1–5 Oct

NEWCASTLE
10–24 Sept

DURHAM 26 Sept

BARNARD CASTLE 29 Sept–5 Oct
YARM 6–13 Oct

NORTHALLERTON
13 Oct

RIEVAULX 13–14 Oct

BATTLE OF
BYLAND

BRIDLINGTON
15 Oct

YORK

The routes taken by the two kings in the weeks prior to the battle. (© Battlefields Trust)

could threaten the Scottish lines of communication if left intact.[9] Bruce was reluctant to leave this formidable squadron in his rear, and had shrewdly delayed crossing the border until it had been dismissed from the King's service at the end of September.

As soon as Harclay's troops were dispersed, the Scots at once began to lay waste and plunder the district around Carlisle, making it impossible for Harclay to regroup his forces, and forcing him to retreat south into Lancashire, in order to muster fresh levies.[10]

It was the speed and mobility of the Scottish army which made it so difficult for their opponents to counter effectively. A Flemish chronicler who served with the English in a later border campaign described the Scots' aptitude for this type of warfare with undisguised admiration -

> *"These Scots are exceedingly hardy through their constant wearing of arms and experience in combat. When they enter England they will in a single day and night cover twenty-four miles; for they ride on sturdy horses and bring no wagons with them. They carry no provisions of bread and wine: for their abstemiousness is such that they will live for a long time on stewed meat and drink river water. They need neither pots nor pans for wherever they invade they find plenty of cattle and use the hides of these in which to boil the flesh. Each man carries under the flap of his saddle an iron plate and behind the saddle a little bag of oatmeal. When they have eaten the stewed meat they place the plate on the fire and when the plate is hot they spread on it a little paste made of oatmeal and water and make a thin cake in the manner of a biscuit which they eat to comfort their stomachs. So it is no wonder that they can travel farther in a day than other soldiers."*[11]

Meanwhile in the east, blissfully unaware of this burgeoning danger, Edward had also dismissed the larger part of what remained of his army, releasing those most badly affected by their recent trials in Scotland and who would be of little use to him militarily. Despite this, it is inconceivable that he did not retain a force large enough to ensure his personal safety while he remained in the vicinity of the Scottish border and within reach of his extremely mobile foes. He kept several of his great retainers with him, including Ralph, Baron Neville, Keeper of the March, Hugh Despenser the Younger, and John de Bermingham, newly created Earl of Louth, each of whom would have had a substantial personal retinue.[12]

Nonetheless, the English king lost no time in attempting to replenish the strength of his army. He had reached Newcastle on the 10th of

The castle of Newcastle. On 20th September 1322 King Edward issued urgent orders to "eight earls and thirty-three others" to join him at Newcastle "...with horses and arms and footmen in as much power as possible...". (CC A-S 3.0 Misaochan)

September, and remained there until the 24th, during which time he caused the following order to be issued -

> 'September 20. Newcastle-on-Tyne.
> To John de Britannia, Earl of Richmond.
>   Order to come with horses and arms and footmen in as much power as possible to the King at Newcastle on the eve of St. Luke next, to set out with the King against the Scotch rebels, who have entered the realm and besieged Norham Castle.
>   By order of the King'[13]

This order was also sent to *"...eight earls and thirty-three others."*

On the same day a similar summons was sent to Andrew de Harcla, Earl of Carlisle, ordering him to come to the King *'...with all the fencible horsemen and footmen, suitably armed... in the counties of Cumberland, Westmoreland, and Lancaster, and in the parts of Cravene and Rychmundshire...'*[14]

Having thus set in train the reinforcement of his army, Edward made a leisurely progress south. Leaving Newcastle on the 24th, he was at Durham on the 26th, and reached Barnard Castle on the 29th of September, where he remained until the 5th of October. It seems it was at this point that intelligence began to reach him of the Scots' movements, and that the Scottish king had crossed the border in the West March. On hearing this news he decided it would be prudent to retreat south-east into Yorkshire, and urgently sent word to ten northern lords to meet him there with further reinforcements -

"Order to bring to the king at Blakhoumor with all speed possible all the horsemen and footmen, suitably armed,... between the ages of sixteen and sixty, the king proposing to

Edward II stayed at Durham on 26th September on the retreat from his invasion of Scotland. (CC 2.0 Gareth Milner)

collect his army at Blakhoumor to repel the Scotch rebels, who have entered the realm in the marches of Carlisle."[15]

It is possible to detect a tone of added exigency in these dispatches, as witness the following addendum, which is absent from similar orders issued barely two weeks earlier from Newcastle -

"He is ordered to cause all persons disobeying him in this behalf to be punished as rebels and aiders of the Scots, for which purpose the King commits him full power."[16]

The exact location of the 'Blakhoumor' referred to in the order is not shown on any modern maps, but has been identified by Professor Barrow as being *"... a locality in the region of Old Byland."*[16] (i.e., the village

Barnard Castle. It was from here on 5th October 1322 that King Edward sent orders to the northern lords for urgent reinforcements. (Author)

situated between Rievaulx Abbey and Sutton Bank). Perhaps Edward chose that locale to assemble his reinforcements because, according to the Lanercost Chronicle, it had hitherto been inaccessible to the Scots - *"...he (Bruce) marched into England to Blackmoor, wither he had never gone before nor laid waste those parts, because of their difficulty of access,..."*[18]

By the 13th Edward had reached Rievaulx Abbey (probably not Byland Abbey as reported by some chroniclers, due to an understandable confusion with Old Byland) to await the arrival of the summoned reinforcements.

Meanwhile, after 5 days of ravaging the lands around Carlisle, reports reached the Scottish king of Edward's whereabouts, and of his planned muster at 'Blackmoor' - *"...having learned for a certainty from his scouts that the King of England was there."*[19]

Displaying all his typical decisiveness and speed of action, Bruce suddenly struck south-east through the Eden valley and Wensleydale, and after covering more than 100 miles in 7 days the army reached Northallerton around the 12th October, a mere 15 miles from Edward at Rievaulx. The march of the Scots from Carlisle to the Vale of Mowbray was a remarkable military exploit, and the speed with which it was achieved caught the English by surprise and ill-prepared.

Wensleydale. Probable route of the Scottish army on its march from Carlisle to Northallerton. (Author)

The Vale of Mowbray from Whitestone Cliff. (Author)

To successfully move a sizeable formation such a long distance, through enemy territory and a hostile populace, and over difficult terrain in uncertain weather conditions, is a testimony not only to the generalship and confidence of the King and his captains, but also to the morale, discipline and experience of the individual soldiers. The army which prepared to face the English was a well-armed, and cohesive fighting force, battle-hardened by a hundred encounters. A formidable and intimidating foe.

It is likely that Scottish armies engaged in raiding England were fully mounted, which afforded them great speed, range and mobility. In the main they were mounted infantry rather than cavalry, as they generally dismounted when confronting the enemy, as we see at Myton and Byland. It seems that each soldier had at least two horses,[20] with the additional mounts serving as a both a spare (the consequences of finding yourself deep in English territory without a horse were serious) and for transporting plunder.

If, as is clearly suggested by the Lanercost Chronicle, Bruce had been informed by scouts of Edward's location there, it seems certain that his plan was to capture some important members of the English court, perhaps even the King himself, with the intention of using them as bargaining counters to force a negotiated settlement. This hypothesis is borne out by the presence on the eve of the battle of another Scottish force at Malton 15 miles south-east of Rievaulx, which perhaps suggests a co-ordinated pincer-movement. This second force may have been shadowing Edward all the way south since his withdrawal from Scotland, or perhaps detached from the main Scottish army on the march from Carlisle, with orders to swing around the North York Moors and get behind Edward's position.[20]

On the 13th, to his great alarm, word reached Edward that the enemy was at Northallerton, and the realisation must have dawned on him that this time their object was not mere plunder and extortion, but no less than an attempt to capture his person. He had been regrouping his army since his muster-call 8 days earlier, and among those who had already joined him with their forces were John of Brittany the Earl of Richmond, the Earl of Louth, and Sir Henry de Beaumont, although for reasons still speculated on he had not been joined by Harclay, who had gathered a significant force, but remained west of the Pennines in Lancashire.

From Rievaulx Edward urgently issued further summons to other magnates to join him immediately, including Aymer de Valance, the Earl of Pembroke, whom he ordered thus -

> *"The K. to the Earl of Pembroke. Understanding from his spies that the Scots are around [North] Allerton, commands the Earl to collect his forces and raise the country towards Byland, reaching it by Thursday the 14th as early in the day as possible, where he will find the Earl of Richmond and Henry de Beaumont, with instructions how to act. The K. is near hand in safety collecting his forces."*
> *13th October, 'the hour of vespers, Rivaux.'[21]*

Pembroke and his forces must have been in very close proximity to the main English army, as Edward fully expected that this order, issued in the evening (vespers), would be complied with the following day, as indeed it was.

The exact numbers that each side was able to bring to the contest is unknown, and remains subject to some speculation, and indeed

Aymer de Valence and Robert Bruce were long-term protagonists, meeting in battle no fewer than 5 times. (© National Library of Wales)

disagreement. Certainly the Scots would have had nowhere near the 80,000 cited by Barbour – a gross exaggeration even for a medieval chronicler. Even if, as Lanercost states, *"The King of Scotland collected all his forces"*,[22] it is impossible that the Scots (or even the English) could have mustered anything remotely near that figure., Sir Thomas Grey also writes that Bruce *"...caused to assemble the whole power of Scotland,..."*,[23] but what number might 'the whole power of Scotland' equate to in the field?

There is something of a consensus among most historians that at the much better-known and closely studied Battle of Bannockburn, the Scottish army was in the region of 5 to 6,000. Professor Barrow argues convincingly that a medieval nation with a total population of around 400,000, as was early 14th century Scotland, could expect to put no more than 10,000 fighting men in the front line. Given that in 1314 Bruce was still not in control of all of Scotland, and that he still had significant domestic opponents, a figure of 6,000 seems a reasonable estimate.[24]

If we move forward to 1322, we find a ruler who is now undisputed ruler of his entire kingdom, and able to marshal its entire resources in support of its military efforts. He has had eight years since Bannockburn to build on that success, and to expand, train and equip his army, largely funded, ironically, by plunder and extortion taken from the north of England. These factors have to be offset by significant losses incurred during the costly expedition in Ireland (1315-18), but considering all aspects it is not unreasonable to believe that the Scottish army may have numbered around 8 to 10,000 men in total at the beginning of the campaign.

It would have been necessary to leave a force of sizeable strength in the eastern march, in order to keep a watching brief on the retreating English army, therefore the number that crossed the border with Bruce may have been much less than this. If, as suggested above, a significant force was detached from the main body en route from Carlisle, with orders to circle around the North York Moors in an effort to trap a retreating Edward, the size of the Scottish army that approached Sutton Bank on the 14th of October is likely to have been in the region of 5 to 6,000, but in the absence of firm evidence this is speculation, albeit informed by sound reasoning.

Skipton Castle. The town of Skipton suffered regularly at the hands of the Scots, in 1318, 1319, and again in the wake of the Battle of Byland. (Author)

It is equally difficult to estimate the English strength, which has been the subject of widely varying estimates over the years. None of the ancient chronicles mention a number for the English forces, save Lanercost, which states that Andrew de Harcla raised 30,000 men in Lancashire. This is surely a greatly inflated number, and in any case a moot point as he did not join the King with his troops until after the battle and the Scots had departed. However, exaggeration or not, it does prove that substantial forces could still be raised, even from territory recently ravaged by the Scots, and therefore it is entirely plausible that Edward could have gathered a large army prior to the battle.

Sir Thomas Grey states that King Edward, *"...perceiving his* (Bruce's) *approach, marched into Blackhow Moor with all the force he could muster..."*[25] – hardly the action of a man heavily outnumbered.

The Scottish sources are equally unhelpful. Barbour merely states that Edward lay at Byland *"...with a strong force,..."*, while Fordun says *"But Edward II, King of England, came against him* (Bruce) *at Biland, with a great force..."*[26]

Attempts to estimate the size of the English army have been skewed in the past by a tendency of some historians to down-play both the size and the significance of the Battle of Byland, with a few commentators dismissing the action as a mere skirmish. Some general histories of the period afford only one or two lines to the battle, or fail to mention it at all. Given the comprehensive nature of Edward's defeat, and the fact that it took place deep within his borders, it is perhaps understandable why English writers might wish to portray it as being against overwhelming odds or of little importance – understandable, but not in keeping with the evidence.

Of what remained of the vast army mustered for the invasion of Scotland, the great majority had been disbanded after recrossing the border, although it is certain that Edward would have retained a sufficient number to guarantee his personal safety. As we have already seen, over the three weeks prior to the battle he had been demanding reinforcements from his retainers across the north of England, and no doubt those forces would have been steadily gathering around his banner at 'Blakhoumor' (Old Byland) in the days leading up to the battle.

In addition, the summons had been sent further afield, with an order sent on the 20th of September to Sir Oliver de Ingham and five others, to bring men to the King from Lincolnshire, Nottinghamshire, and

Edward II from the Choir
Screen in York Minster.
(Author)

Derbyshire, and it is fair to assume that at least some of those levies
would have reached the muster point by the time the Scots arrived at
Northallerton.[27]

We know that by the 13th a number of the great lords were already
in attendance on Edward with their power and that others, including
the Earl of Pembroke, were close by. Each of these magnates would
have a considerable number of men in their households. For example
we know that the Earl of Louth alone had 74 mounted men-at-arms,
115 hobelars, and an unspecified number of footmen in his service.[28] It
is likely therefore that the personal retinues of the King and his nobles
alone would have numbered several thousands, even before the general
levies and militia are counted.

Edward's scouts and spies were no doubt keeping him fully
informed of Bruce's movements and the numbers of the Scottish host,
so the fact that he did not immediately flee on discovering that the Scots

were in such close proximity on the 13th suggests that he had sufficient confidence in the size of his army and the strength of his position. Taking Edward's character into consideration, and judging from his military career as a whole, it is surely inconceivable that he would have risked his interests, indeed his personal safety, to the fortunes of battle had he not had a preponderance of strength sufficient to give him confidence in the outcome. This suggests an English force greater than that of King Robert, perhaps considerably greater, in the region of 8 to 10,000. The suggestion, made by some commentators, that the English army was only a few hundred strong, is certainly wrong.

However, if the English had the ascendancy in terms of raw numbers, in the critical factors of experience, leadership and morale, the advantage lay with the Scots, as subsequent events were to prove.

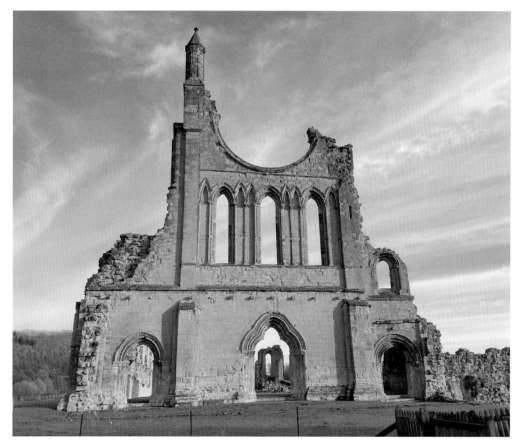

Byland Abbey. (Author)

Chapter 9

The Battle of Byland

Many theories have been put forward over the years as to how the battle unfolded and its exact location, and in this regard it is no different from many other medieval encounters. Every commentator has their own version and this is reflected in the fact that the battle itself has been referred to by various different names, for example the Battle of Old Byland, the Battle of Byland Moor, the Battle of Byland Abbey, the Battle of Scotch Corner, the Battle of Scawton Moor, and perhaps the most geographically accurate, the Battle of Sutton Bank.

The following interpretation is based on a thorough examination of the contemporary and near-contemporary accounts and historical documents, a careful study of the careers of the main protagonists involved, hundreds of hours walking the ground and observing the topography, while also taking into consideration the opinions of other historians. As with all historical study, the conclusions are a subjective analysis, albeit informed by what evidence is available.

1. The initial Scottish assault up the narrow pass

In line with his plan to capture the English king, Bruce made a forced march overnight from Northallerton, hoping to catch the English unaware and to surprise Edward. As Barbour describes -

> *"So that by morning when day came they had come into open country, just a short distance from Byland, but between them and it there was a rocky brae, stretching some distance, with a broad path to go up it. There was no other way for them to go to Byland Abbey except by a very roundabout road."*[1]

Any survey of the local topography reveals that the 'rocky brae' referred to can only be the imposing escarpment of the Hambleton Hills, which rises like a vast wall from the Vale of Mowbray to the west, and the location of the action described by Barbour is surely Sutton Bank,

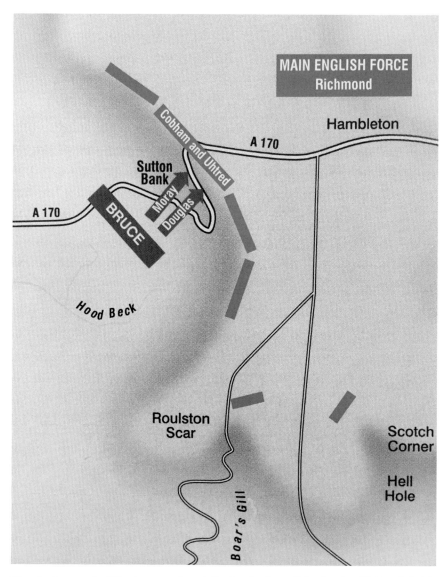

The deployment of the two armies at the beginning of the battle. (© Battlefields Trust)

at the point where the modern A170 snakes up the steep face of the plateau.

In medieval times, as today, the road at Sutton Bank was a key transport intersection. It lay at the point where three important routes met – Hambleton Street, the old drovers' road running north to south along the western edge of the North York Moors - High Street,

A Scottish silver penny of King Alexander III, c. 1286. This coin was discovered in the vicinity of the battlefield in a location consistent with the known movements of the Scottish army. (© York Museum Trust)

heading south-east towards Malton - and Sperragate, the ancient east-west route from Helmsey and Rievaulx Bridge. All three highways converged at an ancient waymarker called Cooper Cross, (Historic England; List Entry Number 1010348), before dropping down to the lowlands of the Vale of Mowbray via the steep path at Sutton Bank, the only accessible passage of the escarpment for miles in either direction.[2]

Cooper Cross stems from early medieval times, and is still there today, situated on the north side of the A170 as it passes the North York Moors National Park Visitor Centre at the top of Sutton Bank (SE 51570 82994). Although only the base and socket still remain, it suggests that the medieval pass where the battle was fought followed the same path that the A170 does today as it descends from the escarpment - strong evidence for locating the battle.[3]

It was the obvious route for the Scots to take in pursuit of their intended target, but unfortunately for them it was equally obvious to the English that it was a key, and eminently defensible position.

We know that English reinforcements were still arriving right up to the last minute. The Earl of Richmond, together with the other English captains, would have been attempting to organise and integrate the recent and new arrivals into their existing forces. They would have wanted as much time as possible to marshal their men into a strong and cohesive formation.

Gormire Lake from White Mare Crag. The Scottish army would have deployed south of the lake before the attack up Sutton Bank. (Author)

With fresh troops expected throughout the day in response to the King's summons, it would make perfect military sense to post a strong division in advance of the main army, to prevent the Scots gaining the high ground and deploying on the plateau. It seems that Edward himself (not so lacking in personal courage as some commentators make out), moved from his base at Rievaulx Abbey to an advanced position at Byland Abbey, in order to be closer to events, which also explains why some chroniclers have him headquartered there.[4]

Bruce clearly hoped that his rapid advance under cover of darkness would take the enemy by surprise, and that the heights of Sutton Bank would be unprotected, or only lightly defended. Instead, as he and

On the morning of the battle King Edward established his forward headquarters at Byland Abbey in order to be closer to events. (Author)

his men approached Sutton Bank at daybreak, they saw banners and pennants fluttering in the wind, and the gleam of the early light on shields and spear-points, which announced that the English were fully alert and prepared. They had placed an advance-guard of their best men on the near-impregnable position along the top of the ridge, and this strong detachment was led by two able captains – Sir Thomas

Ughtred of Scarborough, Constable of Pickering Castle, and Sir Ralph de Cobham, renowned as the bravest knight in the realm, according to Barbour -

> *"For this same Sir Ralph Cobham had the name in all England of the best knight of that land;"*[5]

Faced with this formidable obstacle, King Robert held a hasty council of war with Sir James Douglas, 'the Black Douglas', Thomas Randolph, Earl of Moray, and his other captains, in which they considered the challenging dilemma that lay before them. Any attack on such a well-defended redoubt, accessible only by a precipitous and narrow pass, would be extremely difficult. It would risk serious casualties, take

Pickering Castle. Sir Thomas Ughtred was the Constable of this royal fortress, and mentioned by the ancient chroniclers for his conspicuous bravery in the Battle of Byland. (Author)

considerable time, and offer no guarantee of success. On the other hand, the only way to circumvent the narrow pass was a lengthy 18-mile detour to the south and east by way of Helmsley, which would mean any chance of capturing the prize of Edward and his entourage would certainly be lost. Despite the risks, the Scottish commanders decided that an attempt must be made to carry the position directly by assault, if their plan to seize the English king was to have any chance of succeeding.[6]

This daunting task fell to Douglas and his division, but as he readied his troops for the onslaught he was joined at the head of his men by Moray who, accompanied by four of his squires, chivalrously chose to share the danger with his old comrade-in-arms, and together they led the attack up the steep and narrow pass with the utmost resolution.[7]

However, they were met with equal determination by the English defenders, who put up a spirited and stout resistance -

> *"There you could see men attacking very strongly, others defending themselves by fighting stoutly and arrows flying in great numbers, while those who were above tumbled stones down on the Scots from the high ground."*[8]

'The Black Douglas' as he may have appeared at the Battle of Byland. (Dean Davidson © 3 Swords Historical Services)

105

A Scottish spearman as he may have appeared at the Battle of Byland. (© Diane Lee)

A depiction of an English archer of the period. According to Barbour there were "*...arrows flying in great numbers,*" in the fight at Sutton Bank. (© Diane Lee)

It must have been a desperate and hotly-contested struggle. Neither side was able to bring great numbers to bear in the narrow confines of the steep pass, and bitter hand to hand combat ensued as the Scots manfully pressed the attack in the face of determined opposition. Both Ughtred and Cobham are singled out for praise by the chroniclers for their heroic efforts -

> *"They were both full of great courage, meeting their foes very manfully, but they were strongly pressed."*[9]

Despite the difficulty of the terrain, and the tenacity and courage of the defenders, the battle-hardened veterans of the Scottish spearhead inched their way uphill, gradually forcing the English back by the skill and ferocity of their offensive. But progress was hard-fought and slow, and with every passing minute the chances of taking the English king diminished.

2. The flanking of the English position

It was at this point that King Robert, ever the skilful tactician, played his master-stroke. Seeing that the English were hard-pressed and preoccupied with repelling the Scottish frontal assault, he detached a strong body of troops to circle round and ascend the precipitous slopes at a point hidden from the defenders by the protruding cliffs. The men chosen for this task were mainly from the Highlands of Scotland, and being well used to operating in such difficult terrain they were soon able to gain the ridge which was now more lightly defended as men had been drawn off to help repulse the main attack at Sutton Bank. They quickly overwhelmed their surprised opponents and began to form up in numbers on the English left flank, most likely on the level ground of the plateau, in the area occupied today by the Yorkshire Gliding Club.

Comparing the topography to the accounts leads to the conclusion that the flanking troops would have moved south then west around the base of the cliffs, their movements likely screened by the wooded landscape[10], and that the rocky outcrop they climbed could only be the massive bluff of Roulston Scar. There are two steep gullies on the southern flank of Roulston Scar which fit the description of the access routes used by the agile Highlanders, Hell Hole, and Boar's Gill, where the famous White Horse of Kilburn stands today.

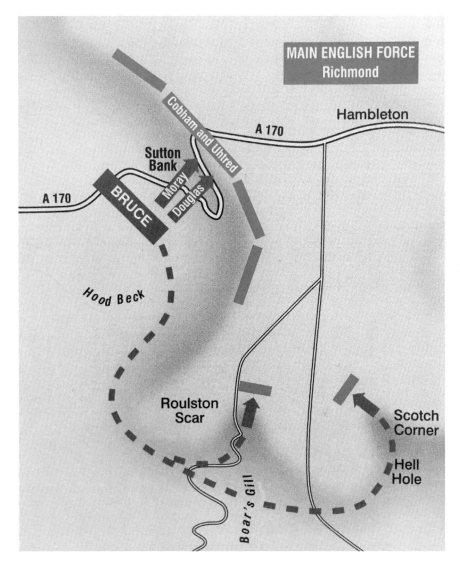

The route taken by the Scots to flank the English position. (© Battlefields Trust)

We might well imagine that Hell Hole may have been given its name by traumatised locals as the place where a horde of strangely dressed clansmen emerged uttering their fierce war-cries, but of more certain significance is the location near the top of the gully of a spot known to this day as Scotch Corner, surely further evidence that this is in fact the route taken by the Scots on their ascent.

Hell Hole, looking south from Scotch Corner. One of the likely routes the Scots used to climb Roulston Scar and flank the English position. (Author)

The chapel at Scotch Corner, situated half-way up Hell Hole, a steep gully on the south-eastern side of Roulston Scar, and one of the routes taken by the Scottish soldiers to reach the high ground. (Author)

It is difficult to say with any certainty if this flanking manoeuvre was undertaken as a result of the King reacting to the unfolding situation, or was part of a premeditated and co-ordinated plan. Certainly, as he had demonstrated on numerous occasions in the past, he was capable of great tactical insight, and able to take decisive action in critical situations. It may be that his decision was taken on the spur of the moment as he watched Douglas and Moray struggle for momentum in the fight at Sutton Bank, in the realisation that the attack was taking too long.

However, there are two main factors in believing that the stratagem had been carefully planned in advance. The first is King Robert's acknowledged generalship and tactical awareness, which surely would have told him that the English position was well-nigh unassailable, and would be extremely difficult, if not impossible, to carry by a frontal assault alone. This in itself would suggest the flanking attack was always part of the plan. Secondly, the circumstances of the battle were almost exactly the same as the situation Bruce found himself some fourteen years earlier, at the Battle of the Pass of Brander in 1308. In that encounter he faced an enemy in a strong defensive position, on higher ground and on a narrow, confined front. On that occasion he triumphed by deploying nimble and lightly-armed men to flank the enemy over difficult terrain. It is highly unlikely that the King did not recognise the similarities and resolve to use the same successful tactics once more.[11]

According to Barbour, the Scots who were attacking up Sutton Bank had just managed to force their way to the top at the same time as their compatriots appeared on the defenders' left flank. Suddenly what had been a difficult position for the English became an impossible one.

3. The rout of the main English force on the plateau

This was the critical moment of the battle. The determination of those defending the pass was already wavering as the attackers relentlessly forced their way up the pass and out on to the level ground. First Cobham was compelled to withdraw in the face of unremitting pressure, with Ughtred, to his great renown, fighting on until overpowered and captured.[12] Then, when a shout went up that the enemy was also bearing down on their flank in force, the resolve of the English broke, and they fled in disorder, seeking sanctuary with their main force somewhere in the vicinity of Cold Kirby and Old Byland. The Lanercost Chronicle describes the scene -

> *"the Scots forced their way fiercely and courageously against them; many English escaped by flight and many were made prisoners,... "*[13]

It was probably around this point that Edward, discovering that the day was going badly, and that the Scots were now too close for comfort, decided to withdraw from his exposed forward position at Byland Abbey to the relative safety of Rievaulx,[14] in order to assess the unfolding situation and take stock. However this 'safety' was to prove illusory as events would quickly prove.

The men of Douglas' division quickly joined with the Highlanders to secure their bridgehead at the summit of the defile, with the rest of the army rushing up the pass to deploy in battle formation on top of the escarpment. Speed was of the essence at this critical juncture, and as soon as they were formed up Bruce immediately ordered his men on to the attack before the English could regroup and restore order to their ranks. The Scots were a well-drilled, battle-hardened and disciplined force, with many years' experience of rapid, mobile warfare to draw on, and with barely a pause for breath they pressed on to the attack.

Reinforcements had been steadily joining the English army over recent days, and more will have been arriving throughout the 14th even as the advance guard was contesting the heights with the Scots. While these additional numbers were no doubt welcome, it must have made it difficult for the Earl of Richmond (Edward's field-commander) to integrate them into his formations, and marshal his troops into an effective fighting force. Given that the first-rank and most experienced soldiers had been levied earlier in the year for the abortive invasion of Scotland, it is likely that many of these new recruits would have been of lesser quality, inexperienced, and probably reluctant to be there.

Richmond and the other English commanders would no doubt have been counting on the defenders of the pass to buy valuable time while they instilled some order and morale into their army, or indeed to prevent the Scots gaining the plateau at all, forcing them instead into a lengthy

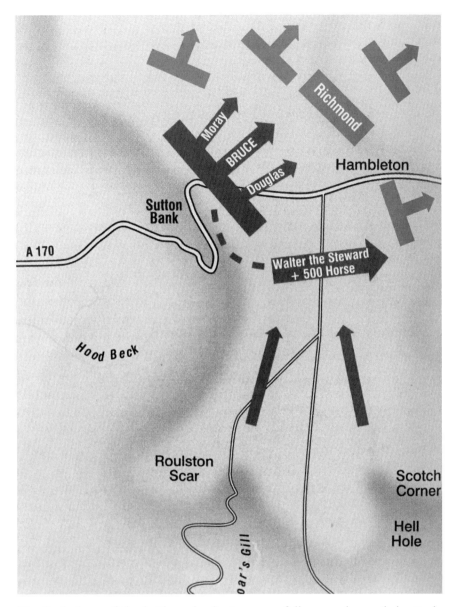

The final phase of the battle – the Scots successfully press home their attack.
(© Battlefields Trust)

and drawn-out detour. It therefore must have come to him as something of an unpleasant shock to see the shattered remnants of his advance guard streaming in panic and disorder towards his lines, and to realise that Bruce was about to fall on his position with his entire army.

Sword pommel, decorated with the arms of the Earl of Richmond. (© Metropolitan Museum of Art NY)

It is easy to imagine the fear and panic that would have swept the ranks of the inexperienced and deflated English host. Despite this, Richmond, it seems, made a valiant effort to stand his ground -

> *"There was a dangerous combat there, for a knight called Sir John Brittany* (The Earl of Richmond) *who was dismounted above the brae, put up a stout defence with his men. Scotsmen attacked them so, and fought so desperately with them, that they were demoralised so that those who could fled away."*[15]

After this spirited but brief struggle, all resistance melted away, and the English army disintegrated in flight, as one English chronicler puts it -

> *"But the Scots were so fierce and their chiefs so daring,
> and the English so badly cowed, that it was no otherwise
> between them than as a hare before greyhounds."*[16]

If the majority of the English army saved themselves by flight, it is also clear they suffered considerable casualties, with many slain or captured -

> *"...many English escaped by flight and many were made
> prisoners,..."*[17]

> *"...but he (Edward II) was put to flight..., in the heart of his
> own kingdom, not without great slaughter of his men, and
> in no little disorder."*[18]

> *"Sir John Brittany was taken there, and a great many of his
> folk were slain."*[19]

By any yardstick it was a heavy defeat for the English, in terms of numbers captured and slain, in terms of Edward's strategic ambitions towards Scotland, and in terms of morale and national pride.

4. The flight and pursuit of King Edward

There is some dispute as to the whereabouts of King Edward during the battle, with some sources placing him at Rievaulx Abbey (Lanercost; Scalaronica; Cal. Docs. Sco.), others at Byland Abbey (Barbour; Gesta; Fordun.) Barbour makes a reference to him as being based at '*Bilandis abbay*', but this is likely to be an error, and the text makes more sense if taken as 'Old Byland. There is clear evidence that he was quartered at Rievaulx, and he was certainly there before and after the battle. As stated above the most plausible scenario is that he was in fact to be found in both locations during the day as events unfolded. Once the Scots had gained the high ground of the plateau, he would no doubt have been hustled back to Rievaulx for his personal security, and to gather his household effects before retreating further to safety. However he was almost undone by the speed of the Scots.

While the Scottish army was assembling on top of the escarpment before advancing to engage their foe, King Robert detached a force of 500 swift

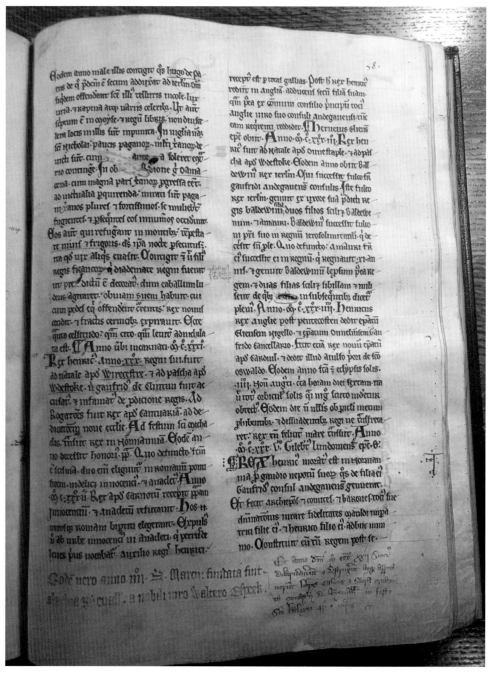

A page from the recently discovered 13th C. manuscript of Roger de Hoveden's (Roger of Howden) 'History of England', which was in the library of Rievaulx Abbey at the time of the battle. (© The Masters of the Bench of the Inner Temple)

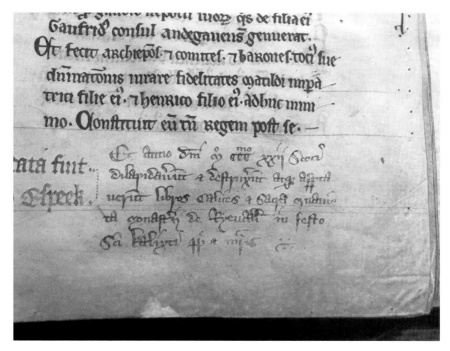

A detail from the page reveals a contemporary annotation written in the margin by one of the monks which translates - *"In the Year of Our Lord 1322 the Scots despoiled and damaged the monastery of Rievaulx, and carried off books, chalices and sacred ornaments, on the feast of St. Callixtus"* (14th October). (© The Masters of the Bench of the Inner Temple)

light horse under the command of his son-in-law Walter the Steward, with the express task of capturing the English king.[20] Acting on intelligence of Edward's location, the Steward and his men swung south around the southern flank of the enemy position, and galloped straight for Rievaulx Abbey, hoping to surprise the retreating monarch and secure his person.

It seems that Edward had barely arrived at Rievaulx from Byland Abbey when news reached him that the Scots were close on his tail -

> *"When this became known to the King of England, who was then in Rievaulx Abbey, he, being ever chicken-hearted and luckless in war and having already fled in fear from them in Scotland, now took flight from them in England, leaving behind him in the monastery in his haste his silver plate and much treasure. Then the Scots, arriving immediately after, seized it all..."*[21]

117

It was only by good fortune that Edward evaded capture, and so precipitous was his flight from Rievaulx that for the second time in his reign he allowed the Great Seal of England to fall into the hands of the Scottish king[22] (who chivalrously returned it a few days later).

For once Edward managed to out-fox his rivals. Instead of heading directly for the safety of York, he, or those of his close entourage advising him, correctly reasoned that he would not be able to outpace the swiftly mounted Scots over any distance, so struck eastwards instead and headed to the coast in the hope of finding a ship. He brought news of his own defeat to Bridlington by way of Pickering, but finding no ship there he headed south overland via Burstwick and by a circuitous route reached York some days later.[23]

Meanwhile the Steward and his 500 horsemen, finding the bird had recently flown from Rievaulx, understandably assumed their quarry would be headed towards York, and hurried off in that direction in the expectation of overtaking him on the road. Reaching the city later the same day and finding the gates barred against them, they realised by now that Edward had managed to evade them. Lacking the means to assault York's formidable defences with any hope of success, the frustrated Scots spent some time challenging and taunting the city's garrison, before returning to King Robert, who was now established in Edward's former quarters at Rievaulx, and enjoying the hospitality the monks had prepared for the English king.[24]

Above left and above right: Great Seal of Edward II. (Allan Wyon, 1843–1907)

In the immediate aftermath of the Battle of Byland the Scots arrived at York, only to find Bootham Bar closed firmly against them. (Author)

Fountains Abbey. This Cistercian establishment was one of the richest monasteries in England, and as such attracted the attention of the Scots. Archbishop Melton of York reported that a large part of the Scottish army stayed there during the invasion of Yorkshire in 1318, and suffered considerable damage to its property, despite paying a hefty fine. (Author)

Chapter 10

Aftermath

A great number of prisoners worthy of ransom had been taken including the English commander, the Earl of Richmond. For some reason the Earl had aroused the ire of Bruce, who spoke harshly to him and ordered that he be confined under close arrest and held for what was then the huge ransom of £20,000,[1] which took two years to raise. This harsh treatment of a high-ranking prisoner is uncharacteristic of Robert, who was known throughout his career for the highest ideals of chivalry, and is markedly at odds with his generous conduct towards the many captives taken at Bannockburn and other occasions.

It is not known for certain what caused this unusual animosity against Richmond, but it has been suggested it may have been as a result of a disparaging remark made against Bruce's queen, Elizabeth, or because the Earl was known to be an outspoken opponent of any peace settlement which would recognise the legitimacy of Bruce's kingship.[2] Richmond also served as 'Guardian of Scotland' for both Edward I and Edward II, and perhaps some action of his during the tenure of that post may have been the cause of King Robert's particular antagonism. For whatever reason, Bruce upbraided him most vehemently in public -

> *"...saying that if he had not been such a caitiff, he would have bought his disgraceful words dearly; and John miserably begged him for mercy."*[3]

This was in marked contrast with the King's treatment of some high-ranking French knights who had been captured in the battle. These included Sir Henry de Sully, the Butler of France, and the Marshall Bretayn, who had been on an embassy from Charles IV to Edward's court, and had felt honour-bound to fight for their host. The French prisoners were treated as honoured guests, and after some time enjoying

Beverley Minster. The Scots agreed not to burn the town on payment of £400.
(Author)

the King's hospitality, were sent home laden with gifts and without ransom.[4] This courteous and generous conduct is much more in keeping with Robert's normal character, but on this occasion may also have been influenced by a desire to court friendly relations with the king of France.[5]

After their complete victory at Byland, no serious resistance to the Scots remained north of the Humber, and they ventured unopposed further into England than ever before. The army appears to have split into three large raiding parties after the battle, in order to maximise the scope for plunder and extortion. One division, led by the Earl of Moray, penetrated deep into the East Riding, hitherto unmolested by the deprivations of the Scots, and the town and college of Beverley was only saved from the flames by paying the hefty sum of £400[6]-

> *"...to escape being burnt by them in like manner as they had destroyed other towns."*[7]

Most of the monks of Bridlington Priory were evacuated to Lincoln, taking their treasure with them, and those that remained bought off the Scots by paying a ransom and agreeing to billet nine Scottish horsemen with eighteen horses.[8]

Bridlington Priory. King Edward sought refuge here during his precipitous flight from Rievaulx, with the Scots hot on his heels. (CC BY 2.0 Jules&Jenny)

Another force, under the command of King Robert himself from his temporary base at Malton Castle, pillaged the area of the Howardian Hills, and south into the Forest of Galtres towards York, causing wholesale damage. The extent of the devastation is evidenced by subsequent revised parish valuations, showing more than fifty parishes where the value of property had reduced by 50% or more, including Sheriff Hutton, Gilling East, and Huntingdon, almost at the gates of York itself.[9]

Malton and its environs were spared the flames on the payment of 300 marks, but that protection was not extended to the town's castle, which was destroyed when the Scots withdrew north.

The third detachment, probably commanded by the Black Douglas, struck west through Airedale as far as Skipton. Thereafter they made their way north again, regrouping on the way, before crossing the border, rich with the spoils of victory, on the 2nd of November, as recorded by Lanercost -

"...but returned laden with spoil and many prisoners and much booty; and on the Commemoration of All Souls they

Sheriff Hutton Castle. After the battle a division of the Scottish army devastated the Forest of Galtres, pillaging over 50 parishes. (CC BY 3.0 ShaunConway)

entered Scotland, after remaining in England one month and three days."[10]

Before the Scots had even left Yorkshire, Andrew Harclay, Earl of Carlisle, joined King Edward at York with the levies he had raised in Lancashire -

> "...in order to attack the Scots with him and drive them out of the kingdom; but when he found the king all in confusion and no army mustered, he disbanded his own forces, allowing every man to return home."[11]

There is no record of what took place between the two men at York, but it must have been an interesting conversation. It is suggested that

The magnificently vaulted undercroft at Fountains Abbey is a stunning example of English medieval Gothic architecture. This vast storehouse would have provided rich pickings for the Scots raiders. (Author)

Edward would have reproached the Earl for failing to reach him with his forces before the battle, where his presence may have been decisive. Harclay was a pragmatic, no-nonsense character, and may have been less than diplomatic in describing the King's handling of the affair, and of his current state of unpreparedness. Whatever transpired, it was to impact profoundly on subsequent events.

Despite his comprehensive defeat and the disgrace of the ensuing humiliation, Edward did not immediately sue for peace. He was not inclined to recognise Scottish independence or the legitimacy of Bruce's kingship; the outcome that the Scottish king prized above all. The fact that in the aftermath of the Battle of Byland he chose to remain in York, rather than fleeing further south when he had the opportunity to do so, indicates that he had every intention of continuing the struggle. By the beginning of 1323 he was already planning another campaign. Edward of Caernarfon may not have inherited either the political acumen or the military skill of his illustrious forebears, but he was not lacking in the obduracy of the Plantagenets, and his initial response to the catastrophe of Byland was to plan for the continuation of the war.

However, if Edward II was content to continue the struggle, the war-torn communities of northern England clamoured for peace. They despaired of a king who appeared wholly insensitive to their suffering, and who was patently unable to protect them militarily. The debacle of Byland convinced many it was time to take matters into their own hands, including the Archbishop of York, who issued letters authorising the clergy of the archdiocese to enter into local agreements with the Scots, and the Bishop of Durham who entered into direct negotiations with them.[12]

The Earl of Carlisle was another who decided the time had come for unilateral action. His unsatisfactory meeting with the King at York had served only to confirm his disillusionment with the conduct of the war, and with Edward personally. For over ten years he had been engaged in defending the West Marches against the Scots, and had resisted several determined efforts to capture Carlisle. He knew at first-hand the on-going suffering and deprivation endured by the local populace, and with no end in sight he determined to enter into direct negotiations with the Scottish king to secure a lasting peace.

Durham Cathedral. After the defeat at Byland the Bishop of Durham entered into direct negotiations with the Scots, in an effort to obtain some respite for the people of his diocese. (CC 2.0 Gareth Milner)

> *"Wherefore, when the said Earl of Carlisle perceived that the King of England neither knew how to rule his realm nor was able to defend it against the Scots, who year by year laid it more and more waste, he feared at last he [the King] should lose the entire kingdom; so he chose the lesser of two evils, and considered how much better it would be for the community of each realm if each king should posses his own kingdom freely and peacefully without any homage, instead of so many homicides and arsons, captivities, plunderings and raidings taking place every year."*[13]

The two men met at King Robert's castle at Lochmaben on the 3rd of January 1323, and after 'protracted discussions' a treaty was agreed whereby England surrendered all claim to Scotland and recognised Bruce as legitimate King of Scots. In return the Scots undertook to give an annual indemnity of 4,000 marks for ten years and the right to nominate an English bride for King Robert's heir. It was a pragmatic and realistic arrangement, not dissimilar to the treaty eventually agreed in 1328 and, had it been accepted by Edward, would have saved both nations a further five years of conflict.

Harclay may have believed he was negotiating with the authority of a previously issued royal commission under the Great Seal,[14] or his intention may have been to present the English king with a *fait accompli*, but either way his efforts were doomed to failure. Edward's offended pride blinded him to the mutual and obvious benefits of the proposed agreement, and his spiteful and ungrateful character was outraged by what he saw as the Earl's betrayal. Harclay was accused of treason, arrested and tried, and condemned to suffer the full horror of a traitor's

Andrew Harclay, Earl of Carlisle was accused of treason for agreeing a peace treaty with King Robert without royal authority. Despite his past services to Edward II, he was condemned to be hung, drawn and quartered as a traitor. A 14th C. depiction of a man being drawn to execution. (© British Library)

death. Thus died the man who, through his victory at Boroughbridge during the Earl of Lancaster's uprising, had done more than anyone to maintain Edward on his throne, and who in recent years had been England's only effective bulwark against the Scots.[15]

Ironically, Harclay's death contributed indirectly in bringing some respite to northern England, if not the permanent peace he had hoped for. The loss of his ablest captain, and the kingdom's main buffer against the depredations of the Scots, together with a deterioration in relations with France, forced Edward to negotiate. On the 13th May in York the king's council proposed a lengthy truce for thirteen years, which was accepted by Bruce at Berwick on the 7th June under his title of King of Scots. Edward's *de facto* acceptance of King Robert's regal title, together with the other agreed concessions, was a vindication of everything Bruce had been fighting for since he seized the Scottish crown seventeen years previously and served as a precursor to the formal treaty of 1328.[16] It marked the end of an era, and never again in the remainder of his reign would Edward II take up arms against the Scots.

Although not fought on the same scale, in many ways the Battle of Byland was as remarkable a victory as King Robert's triumph in the great set-piece battle at Bannockburn eight years earlier. It was fought deep within enemy territory, and is a case study in the effective combination of logistics, communications and intelligence in a medieval military campaign. His lightning march across the North of England was a *tour de force* rarely matched in the history of our island, and the campaign as a whole served to underline Robert Bruce's genius as a leader of men, a strategist, and tactician.

It is appropriate therefore that a magnificent memorial marker was recently erected on the 700th anniversary of the battle to recognise this landmark achievement in King Robert's illustrious career. The impressive monolith, of rugged unhewn ganister sandstone, stands like a lone sentinel looking out over Sutton Bank and the Vale of Mowbray, and is a fitting monument to the courage and sacrifice of the men from both nations who fought there on that October morning in 1322.

The stone and the adjacent interpretation board were erected as the outcome of a joint project involving the North York Moors National Park, the Battlefields Trust, and the North Yorkshire Moors Association. They were unveiled on the 15th of October 2022 as the centre piece of a day of commemorative events by the author and the Honourable Adam

The Battle of Byland Memorial Stone, erected to mark the 700th anniversary of the battle in 2022. (Author)

Bruce, son of the Earl of Elgin, head of the Bruce family, in the presence of a large and enthusiastic gathering.

It is a travesty that this remarkable military achievement is so little known, even in Scotland where one might expect it to enjoy greater renown. It is the author's hope that the publication of this book may go some way to generating impetus towards rectifying this, and that the Battle of Byland can take its overdue and rightful place in the long venerable history of our island.

Norham Castle occupies a key strategic position overlooking a vital ford over the Tweed. Attacked numerous times by the Scots, it withstood three prolonged sieges between 1318 and 1322. (Tessa Critchlow)

Appendix A

The Treaty of Edinburgh/Northampton

The remainder of Edward II's inglorious reign descended into ever-increasing dissension and civil discord, pitting the King and his unpopular favourites, the Despensers (father and son, both called Hugh), against a baronial party which came to be led by Edward's estranged queen, Isabella, and her confederate and lover Roger Mortimer, one of the chief Marcher Lords. This led to Edward's eventual deposition in January 1327, and the capture and execution of the Despensers. The dethroned king was succeeded by a regime in the name of his 14-year-old son, Edward III, and was to die a horrific death at Berkeley Castle in September 1327 (allegedly by having a red-hot iron thrust into his bowels, in order to leave no mark on his body).[1]

The thirteen-year truce agreed at Bishopthorpe in 1323 had, despite some provocations from the English, been largely observed by both parties, until the forced abdication of Edward. This event had been taken by King Robert as freeing him from all obligations under the truce, and on the 1st February 1327 (the same day as the coronation of Edward III) he launched an attack on Norham Castle. The new regime in England responded by mobilising for war, and a large army was summoned to assemble at York at the beginning of July. This included a detachment of heavily armed and mounted Flemish mercenaries, some 2,500 strong, and hired for the vast sum of £40,000.

Rather than wait to be attacked, the Scots launched a major pre-emptive incursion into England on the 15th of June, led by the now familiar pairing of Moray and Douglas, together with Donald, Earl of Mar. The vast English army lumbered north from York on the 10th of July, nominally led by the young King Edward III, but under the command of Sir Roger Mortimer and John of Hainault.

The tomb of Edward II in Gloucester Cathedral. (Author)

Edward was anxious to 'win his spurs' with a victory over the Scots, but after being given the 'run-around' for over three weeks by the mobile and daring Scots, he was defeated in a skirmish at Stanhope Park, and only narrowly escaped capture himself. It is said he wept tears of frustration as his famished and wasted army withdrew back to York, as once again an English king had been humiliated by an inferior Scottish force in his own country.[2]

Worse was to follow for the English as in August King Robert himself, recently returned from a successful excursion in Ireland, launched a full-scale invasion of Northumberland, and laid siege to the castles of

Norham, Warkworth, and Alnwick. It seemed that Bruce now aimed at permanent annexation, rather than short-term raiding, as he began to grant lands in Northumberland to his followers by charter.[3]

Whether this was a realistic long-term goal, or merely a bargaining stratagem, it had the desired effect. Such a conspicuous display of *de facto* Scottish hegemony over the northern counties, coming so soon after the fiasco of the Stanhope Park campaign, applied great pressure on the ruling regime in England to come to terms. This, together with the increasing financial problems which caused the dismissal of the Hainault mercenaries, and the growing unpopularity of Isabella and Mortimer, combined to force the English government to the negotiating table.

Discussions began in earnest in October 1327, and after much diplomatic manoeuvring and posturing, Edward finally conceded the crucial points before a Parliament convened at York on the 1st of May 1328, and in the presence of the Scottish envoys, as recorded in letters patent to be conveyed to their king -

The final resting place of the heart of Robert Bruce. It was the King's dying wish that, after his death, his heart be removed from his body and carried on crusade. Sir James Douglas undertook to do this, but died fighting the Moors in Spain before reaching the Holy Land. Bruce's heart was recovered from the battlefield and returned to Scotland, and buried here at Melrose Abbey. (Author)

"To all Christ's faithful people who shall see these letters, Edward, by the Grace of God, King of England, Lord of Ireland, Duke of Acquitaine, greeting and peace everlasting in the Lord. Whereas, we and some of our predecessors, Kings of England, have endeavoured to establish rights of rule or dominion or superiority over the realm of Scotland, whence dire conflicts of wars waged have afflicted for a long time the Kingdoms of England and Scotland: we, having regard to the slaughter, disasters, crimes, destruction of churches and evils innumerable which, in the course of such wars, have repeatedly befallen the subjects of both realms, and to the wealth with which each realm, if united by the assurance of perpetual peace, might abound to their mutual advantage, thereby rendering them more secure against the hurtful efforts of those conspiring to rebel or to attack, whether from within or without: **We will grant by these presents, for us, our heirs and successors whatsoever, with the common advice, assent and consent of the prelates, princes, earls, barons and the commons of our realm in our Parliament, that the Kingdom of Scotland, within its own proper marches as they were held and maintained in the time of King Alexander of Scotland, last deceased, of good memory, shall belong to our dearest ally and friend, the magnificent prince, Lord Robert, by God's grace illustrious King of Scotland, and to his heirs and successors, separate in all things from the Kingdom of England, whole, free and undisturbed in perpetuity, without any kind of subjection, service, claim or demand. And by these presents, we denounce and demit to the King of Scotland, his heirs and successors, whatsoever right we or our predecessors have put forward in any way in bygone times to the aforesaid Kingdom of Scotland."**[14]

In simple terms the final treaty, signed separately in Edinburgh and Northampton, recognised the independence of Scotland, and Robert Bruce's right to the throne. There was to be a 'perpetual peace' between the two kingdoms, and this would be consolidated through the marriage of Prince David, the only son of the King of Scots, and Princess Johanna, sister of Edward III. In addition the Scots agreed to pay £20,000, and the English promised to help in having the Papal interdict lifted from Scotland.[5]

When ratified by King Edward and his Parliament in May 1328, the treaty established everything King Robert and his people had striven for through thirty-two years of warfare, struggle and hardship. At the extremity of his life and his reign, Robert Bruce, King of Scots, was finally, and fully, vindicated.[6]

Sadly, the Warrior King did not have long to enjoy the fruits of his labour. Worn out by years in the saddle, exposure to the elements, and untold hardship, he died peacefully in his bed on the 7th of June 1329, surrounded by his old friends and brothers-in-arms.[7]

The tomb of King Robert I 'the Bruce', in Dunfermline Abbey. (CC BY 3.0 Otter)

An aventail. This attached to the helmet, and offered good protection to the early 14th century man-at-arms. (Royal Armouries)

Appendix B

Notes on Early 14th Century Armies

1. The Feudal Levy

For more than two centuries prior to the Battle of Byland, armies in England had been raised according to the tenets of the feudal system as instituted by William I after his successful seizure of the crown in 1066. Under this system the king apportioned land grants, or fiefs, to his vassals (tenants-in-chief) in exchange for specified military service (*servitium debitum* or "service owed"), and this allowed William to reward his chief retainers, settle and pacify the land and consolidate his power base. The tenants-in-chief in turn granted fiefs to the next tier of nobility (mesne tenants), again for a specified level of military support, and the mesne tenants could grant fiefs further down the line, thus creating a huge socio-economic and militaristic pyramid with the king at the apex, from which the Crown derived its wealth and power.

In time of war the king would issue a 'Call to Arms', and the 'Feudal Levy' was raised. Under the Feudal Levy each vassal was expected to provide a certain number of trained soldiers, equipped and ready to fight for a fixed period, usually 40 days (which could be extended to 90 in emergencies). As each soldier had to be clothed, fed and provided with weapons, this could be a costly business. The limited service time was meant to ensure the land would not be neglected entirely in time of war.

The feudal system had also been adopted in Scotland, not by conquest as in England, but because successive 12th century Scottish kings observed its workings south of the border, and saw its benefits for a strong monarchy and centralised government. Throughout the reigns of Edgar (1097 – 1107), Alexander I (1107 – 1124), and particularly David I (1124 – 1153), these (and subsequent) kings actively encouraged the settlement of powerful Anglo-Norman and Anglo-Breton barons and

14th C footsoldier with polearm weapon. (Dean Davidson © 3 Swords Historical Services)

Spears of various lengths were a favoured weapon of the Scottish soldiers. (Dean Davidson © 3 Swords Historical Services)

their various retainers and adherents throughout the south and east of Scotland, thus largely replicating the feudal system within a few short generations.

In the early 1300s the method by which an army was raised would be broadly similar in both nations, but with two important caveats. Firstly, Scotland still retained a significant Gaelic element to its culture, which, although a minority, was a large and influential one. The feudal system had not been embraced in the north-west and the islands, and military service there was still based on family connections and clan loyalty. Secondly, Scotland was vastly inferior to England in terms of land (both in area and quality) and population. With less than a tenth of the manpower and resources available to its richer and more powerful neighbour, such a disparity inevitably affected both the size and make up of the Scottish army.

By the time we reach the early 14th century, national armies in England had begun to rely less on the traditional feudal levy. There are

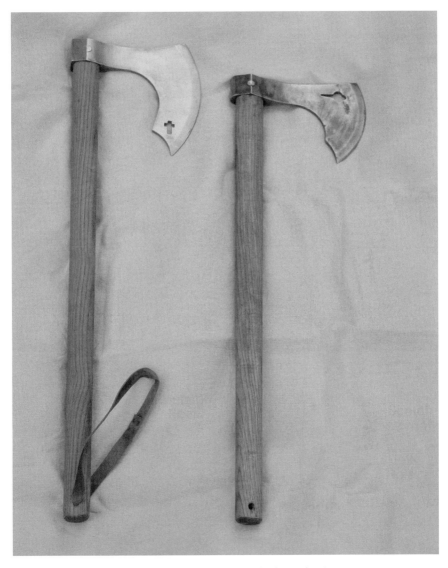

Battleaxes. (Dean Davidson © 3 Swords Historical Services)

various reasons for this development, but the main factor was that the demands facing kings of this era required a military capability that was more reliable and flexible than that provided by the feudal levy alone. At the same time successive kings, notably Edward I, came to believe that military service on behalf of the Crown was the duty of all subjects, not just the king's direct feudal vassals. This concept was formalised in the Statute of Westminster (1285) which required all able-bodied Englishmen between the ages of fifteen and sixty to fight for the realm when the king deemed it necessary.

In practice this potential universal conscription was never fully implemented. Most men could and did commute their military service through a monetary payment, but it provided kings with a mechanism to fund the creation of specialist bodies of troops such as archers and spearmen, to supplement the feudal levy. This development led to the use of paid and contracted forces through a system of military service in return for an annual, fixed payment from the lord (*fief rente* or "indentures of retainer"). These companies could be raised within the king's realm, or from foreign sources, such as Italian crossbowmen or Flemish men-at-arms. These agreements, or 'contracts', were usually oral to begin with, but by the time of the Hundred Years' War formal written indentures were the norm. (note; McKisack pg 225). Some examples of written indentures survive from the early 14th century, such as that of Maurice de Berkeley, who agrees to serve the king for life, with fourteen men-at-arms in time of war.[1] Others were shorter fixed-term agreements, such as one between Edward Montagu and King Edward III in 1341, whereby Montagu undertakes to provide six knights, twenty men-at-arms, twelve armed footsoldiers, and twelve archers, all for the sum of £76.[2]

This 'hybrid' method of raising royal forces is seen throughout the reigns of the first two Edwards, with progressively less reliance on the feudal levy with each muster. The last practical use of the feudal host was that of Edward III in 1327, although a purely symbolic summons was issued by Richard II in 1385. These developments were mirrored in Scotland to a lesser degree (notwithstanding the caveats mentioned above) as fiscal constraints curtailed the widespread use of contracted forces.

Instead King Robert, while maintaining the principle of feudal armed service, altered its emphasis as the situation demanded. As soon as he was in a position to grant tenure, rather than requiring the traditional levy of one armed knight, he instead demanded ten archers. Bruce had most likely been present at the Battle of Falkirk, and had witnessed at first hand the deadly effectiveness of massed archers. Throughout his reign he continued to amend the terms feudal military service required from lessees to suit his needs at any given time. His aim in doing so was to

Sword and shield – the 'essentials' of the 14th C man-at-arms. (Dean Davidson ©
3 Swords Historical Services)

establish a national reserve of trained fighters of all types. An example of
this strategy was a statute he had the Scottish Parliament enact in 1318,
whereby every freeman worth £10 or more was required to provide
himself with a leather gambeson, steel helmet, and steel gauntlets. This
foresight, coupled with the hard school of war, led to the creation of
a well-equipped, disciplined and experienced soldiery, a fighting force

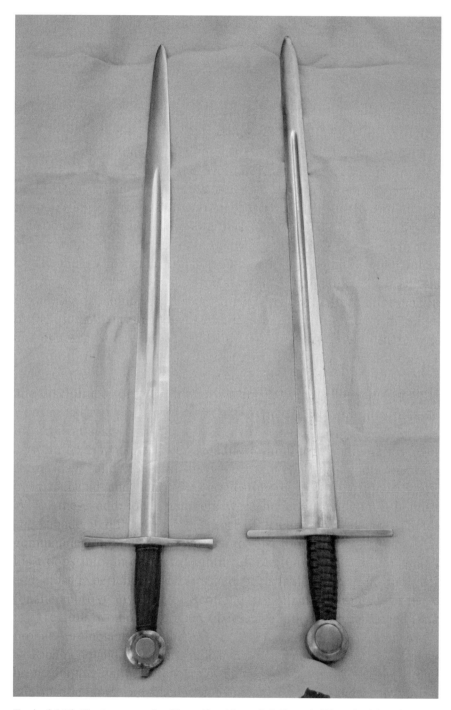

Typical 14th Century swords. (Dean Davidson © 3 Swords Historical Services)

which was able to more than hold its own against a much greater and more powerful adversary throughout more than 20 years of almost constant warfare. It was an army which even earned the admiration of English chroniclers:

> *"Each soldier was furnished with light armour, not easily penetrable by a sword. They had axes at their sides and carried spears in their hands. They advanced like a thick-set hedge, and such a phalanx could not easily be broken."*[3]

In both countries, whether it be under *'servitium debitum'*, or *'fief rente'*, each of the king's retainers was expected to respond to the call to arms with an agreed number and type of soldiers, depending on the size of his tenure. For example we know that in response to King Edward's summons before the Battle of Byland that Sir Henry Percy arrived with 7 knights and a further 49 men-at-arms, together with 48 hobelars (a type of mounted infantry), and Sir Ralph Neville brought 7 knights, 33 men-at-arms, and 80 hobelars.[4]

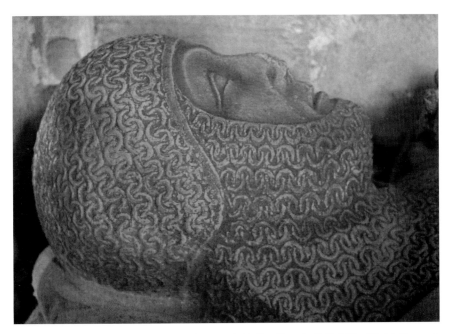

Effigy of Sir William de Cantiloupe d.1309, St Felix Church, Felixkirk. (Keith Dowen)

In addition to the heavily-armed and armoured men-at-arms came a greater number of infantry. As a result of the almost continuous warfare throughout the late 13th and early 14th century, a class of semi-professional troops began to emerge, who were both better armed and more experienced than their forebears, who had been little more than pressed civilians armed with adapted agricultural implements. These foot soldiers were often formed into specialist companies of spearmen or archers, although they also fought with swords and various types of axes. Under special circumstances they could also be mounted on light horses to form more mobile mounted infantry companies (as the examples cited above), but this was exceptional and in general they fought on foot. In the great armies raised by the first two Edwards for the Scottish wars, the ratio of infantry (including archers) to men-at-arms was typically in the ratio of five or six to one.

Although they made up a smaller proportion of the king's forces than the footsoldiers, the mainstay of the English army in 1322 remained the man-at-arms, who was a heavily armoured warrior, proficient in the use of arms, and mounted. (There is some overlap in the use of the terms 'knight' and 'man-at-arms', although they are not strictly synonymous. Though it is correct to say all knights were men-at-arms, not all men-at-arms were knights, which implied a specific social standing. For the purpose of this discussion we will use the terms interchangeably.)

Effigy of Sir Richard de Goldsborough d.1308, Church of St Mary the Virgin, Goldsborough. A well-preserved effigy detailing arms and armour of the period. (Keith Dowen)

The knight would be accompanied by several squires and pages who would look after his personal needs, his arms and armour and his several horses, known as *destriers*. These great war-horses, specially bred for the strength and stamina required to carry a fully-armoured warrior in battle, were an indispensable element in the equipage of the medieval knight and a measure of his standing and prestige. They were enormously expensive, sometimes costing over £100, and just keeping them in fodder during a campaign presented a huge logistical challenge to English armies of the day -

> *"The English do not willingly enter Scotland to wage war before summer, chiefly because earlier in the year they can find no food for their horses"*[5]

At this time in the development of military tactics, the full-scale charge of massed heavily-armed cavalry was still regarded as the primary means to gaining victory, although the man-at-arms would also be able to fight on foot if circumstances required, as seen with Ughtred, Cobham and their company at Sutton Bank.

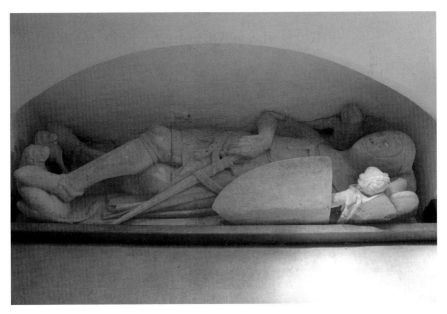

Sir Mauger St. Aubyn d.1320, St George's Church, Georgeham. This effigy shows contemporary armour in great detail. (Keith Dowen)

2. Arms and Armour

Armour of the period was beginning to transition from mail to plate, although most men-at-arms in the first half of the 14th century would still rely on the former as their main body protection.

In 1322 a typical knight may have worn a padded jacket or gambeson, under a mail tunic *or* hauberk which came down to the knees. The head was protected by a mail coif, and the hands by mail mittens or gloves of plate. As armour developed, metal plates were added to mail, protecting the knee and lower leg with greaves, and the upper and lower arm with the rerebrace and vambrace respectively. Vulnerable joints such as the knee, elbow and armpit could be protected by strategically placed roundels.

In close combat the man-at-arms might still use a fully-enclosed 'great helm', but this was gradually being replaced by the close-fitting conical bascinet, with or without a visor. The bascinet was often worn with an aventail attached, a curtain of mail which protected the neck and shoulders. Over their body armour the knightly class would wear a long surcoat, often displaying their coat of arms, so that they could be identified in battle.

For a mounted charge a knight might use a lance, but his main weapon, on horseback or on foot, was the sword, which was becoming longer and heavier as armour improved. Various other weapons were used, including the battleaxe (single and two-handed), mace, and war-hammer.

Above left and above right: An excellent example of an early 14th C. bascinet. Note the fixings for attaching a mail aventail. (© Metropolitan Museum of Art NY)

The common foot-soldier might also use any of these weapons (if he could afford them), sometimes scavenged from battlefield casualties, but pole weapons tended to be favoured. These were originally derived from agricultural and hedging implements, and included the bill, pole-axe, and various lengths of spear. Their armour would also largely depend on what they could afford or acquire, but they tended to eschew heavy armour in favour of agility when fighting.

Some form of quilted gambeson would be typical, with the semi-professional class also using the hauberk or perhaps a coat of scale armour. Head protection varied, with the chapelle-de-fer or 'kettle hat' widely used, although archers tended to prefer the brimless close-fitting iron skull-cap, or simply a padded arming cap. Leg armour was not commonly used as it restricted mobility.

The English army's defeat at Bannockburn in 1314 at the hands of densely packed spearmen alerted King Edward to the need for his footsoldiers to be better armed and protected. Consequently in subsequent musters he attempted to stipulate minimum standards for equipment, and in his levy of 1316 infantry were required to come with aketon (similar to a gambeson), bascinet and lance. In 1318 aketon, hauberk, bascinet and iron gloves, were called for, and in 1319, no doubt in an attempt to match the Scottish army for speed and mobility, soldiers with goods worth between 100s. and 10 marks were also required to bring a horse in addition to these items.[6]

SIR JOHN DE CREKE.
In Westley Waterless Church,
in Cambridgeshire, 1325.
After Waller.

(SIR WILLIAM) FITZ RALPH.
In Pebmarsh Church in Essex, 1323.
After Waller.

Right and far right: Drawings from brass monuments showing typical knights of the period. (Encyclopaedia Britannica, 1911)

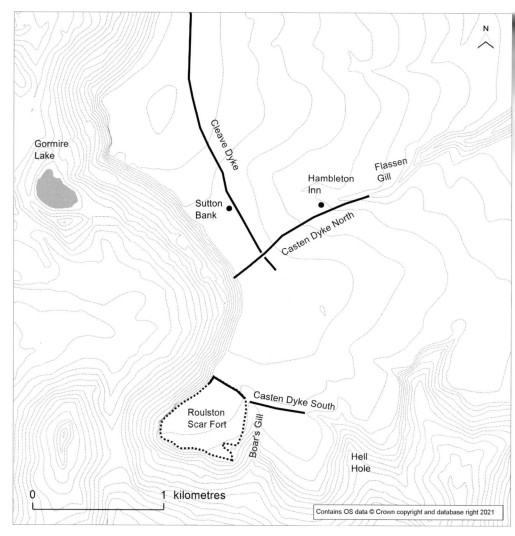

Map of the south western scarp of the Hambleton Hills, showing the main archaeological features including the Late Bronze Age Cleave Dyke system, and the Iron Age promontory fort at Roulston Scar. (Sandra Kennish)

Appendix C

Archaeological Considerations

In recent years the North York Moors National Park Authority has commissioned various archaeological investigations, which have revealed some interesting findings which may be relevant to the study of the battle. In 1996 a survey was carried out on some earthworks at Hambleton above Sutton Bank, known as Casten Dyke North, and previously believed to be prehistoric. Investigations revealed that the dyke had been re-cut in the historic period with defences facing south, with dating consistent with the only known historic event in the area, i.e., the battle of 1322.

Further investigations were conducted in 2001 by English Heritage during a survey of earthworks adjacent to Roulston Scar hillfort, situated just under a mile south of Sutton Bank. As part of this work the earthworks known as Casten Dyke South were examined, and revealed to be a north-facing defensive feature of a historic rather than prehistoric date. Casten Dyke South runs roughly east to west joining the tops of the two steep gullies believed to have been used by the Scots to reach the high ground, namely Boar's Gill and Hell Hole. It protects a promontory of land around 28 hectares in size, of sufficient area to accommodate a sizeable force of men.

The most recent excavation took place in 2013, carried out by the Landscape Research Centre, examining the defensive rampart of Roulston Scar hillfort itself. This revealed a linear trench cut into the existing Iron Age earthworks, with evidence of a palisade, and of a period compatible with the events of 1322. This defensive structure again faces north, and encompasses a roughly triangular area of 24 hectares, with steep cliffs protecting the other two sides, and immediately adjacent on the west to the area protected by Casten Dyke South. The archaeological evidence suggests both sites were in use for only a very short period of time.

These discoveries have led some to speculate that the rival armies had 'dug in' before the engagement, and that the battle was fought from entrenched positions, the Scots behind Casten Dyke North facing south, and the English facing north behind the Roulston Scar defences and Casten Dyke South.

However, this is surely unlikely, as it is at odds with every description of the battle contained in the various chronicles, and goes against everything we know about the speed of the Scots' movement and their well-established and favoured tactics.

It is much more likely that the English army, unsure of the exact location of the Scots, but all too aware of their ability to cover great distances very rapidly, hastily fortified these two easily-defensible positions in the days leading up to the battle, to afford them some safety and a secure base for the reinforcements arriving from various parts. Until greater light is shed by further archaeological evidence, this seems to be a plausible hypothesis as to the function of these defensive earthworks.

Aerial view of Roulston Scar and Sutton Bank from the south. The gully to the right of the White Horse is Boar's Gill, one of the routes used by the Scottish flanking force. (Kimberli Werner)

Appendix D

The battlefield today, and suggested walks

The site of the Battle of Byland lies within the North York Moors National Park, and a visitor centre with parking, toilets and catering facilities is situated at the top of Sutton Bank, just a few yards from the spot where the most intense fighting took place.

The Sutton Bank National Park Centre (YO7 2EH) is just off the A170, 6 miles east of Thirsk, and about 7.5 miles west from Helmsley, and can be reached from York via the A19 in about 45 minutes.

The areas where the various phases of the battle unfolded remain largely undeveloped today, and it is possible to follow the movements of both armies on paths leading from the visitor centre.

There are two recommended 'battlefield' walks, as follows.

Walk 1

This a medium difficulty 5.5 mile (8.9km) circular walk, dropping down the escarpment to the area near Gormire Lake where the Scottish army would have deployed before the battle. Then traversing south beneath Roulston Scar and around below the 'White Horse of Kilburn', following the route taken by the troops sent to circle round the English position. Then ascending Boar's Gill, one of the routes taken by the Scots as they fought their way to the high ground, before tracing the steps of their charge into the flank of the English army defending Sutton Bank.

- Start the walk at the North York Moors National Park Visitor Centre at Sutton Bank.
- Follow the signs to the Finest View in England (according to James Herriot) at 1.

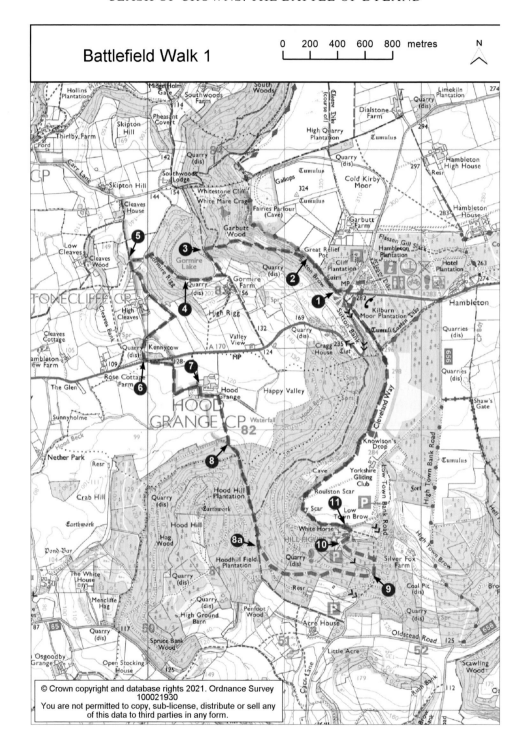

Battlefield Walk 1

0   200   400   600   800 metres

N

- Head North West along the Cleveland Way for a short distance, then at 2 take the path down the escarpment to Garbutt Wood and Lake Gormire at 3.
- Go clockwise round the lake and where the path forks at 4 keep left.
- At the top of the rise bear left, drop down to cross a small stream and a stile, then rise again beside a tall hedge to a footpath running North-South at 5.
- Turn left and follow the footpath signs around High Cleaves house, dropping down to reach the A170 at 6.
- Turn left, keeping on the grass verge. Take care – very busy road! After 50 yards cross the road and follow the footpath down the metalled track leading to Hood Grange at 7.
- Follow the footpath as it skirts to the South of the farm and then heads South up the rise to join the Hood Hill Plantation track at 8.
- Turn left and follow this wide forest track all the way to White Horse Bank at 9. At 8A keep left on the main track; ignore the track leading off to the right.
- At the road cross over (care!) then turn left and follow the path running beside the road, at higher level, before crossing back over the road into the car park at 10.
- Climb the steps beside the White Horse (take your time!) and have a breather at the top 11 while enjoying the views.
- Head West and follow the Cleveland Way round the edge of the escarpment, passing Roulston Scar and the Yorkshire Gliding Club, and return to the Visitor Centre

Shorter variations

For those wishing a shorter outing it is possible to walk sections of the above walk without doing the full circuit.

Shorter Option 1 – Whitestonecliff (approx. 2.5 miles / 4km)

Follow the directions as above until point 2. Instead of dropping down the escarpment, stay on the Cleveland Way heading north for approximately a further 0.6 mile (1km) to Whitestonecliff. (Parts of this route follows an unfenced cliff edge – please keep your dog on a lead at all times on this path). From here there are wonderful panoramic views over the Vale of Mowbray, and looking to the north west it is possible to see the route the Scots would have taken in their march from Northallerton.

There are also magnificent views looking down on Gormire Lake and the area where the Scottish army would have deployed before the assault on Sutton Bank. From here retrace your steps to the visitor centre.

Shorter Option 2 – the White Horse (approx. 3 miles / 5km)

From the visitor centre, carefully cross the A170 at the recommended crossing point, and pause to admire the magnificent memorial stone commemorating the battle, with its very informative interpretation board. From here head south following the signposted path marked 'Cleveland Way, White Horse 1m'. (The route follows an unfenced cliff edge and runs beside the gliding club landing area – please keep your dog on a lead at all times on this path). Looking down to your right you will see where the A170 climbs sharply from the valley below, which is where the fiercest fighting took place in 1322. The path follows the escarpment along the western then southern flank of Roulston Scar, looking down on the route taken by a detachment of the Scottish army on their manoeuvre to outflank the English position. At the White Horse, stay on the top path for a few hundred yards more before reaching Low Town Bank Road and a small car park. The wooded area beyond the car park hides the steep gully called Boar's Gill, which is one of the routes the Scots used to gain the high ground and surprise the English defenders.

From here retrace your steps to the visitor centre.

Walk 2

This is a 6 mile /9.7km (12 mile round trip) linear walk from Sutton Bank to Rievaulx Abbey, which roughly follows the route taken by Walter the Steward and his 500 horsemen as they pursued Edward II from the battle. This path is entirely on the Cleveland Way (apart from the half-mile section from Rievaulx Abbey to Rievaulx Bridge) and is well sign-posted. It can be walked from either direction, with parking and toilets at both ends. The English Heritage site at Rievaulx Abbey is well worth a visit, with well-preserved ruins, cafe, shop and museum. The route passes through the village of Cold Kirby (no facilities) and the area around here and the neighbouring village of Old Byland is believed to be a possible site for the location named as 'Blakhoumor' or 'Blackmoor' in various ancient chronicles, where the main English army mustered before the battle.

Map

OS Explorer: OL26 North York Moors, Western Area.

Battlefield Walk 2

Old Byland, the probable site of the location described as 'Blakhoumor' or 'Blackmoor' in various ancient documents. It is likely the main English force was deployed in this vicinity. (Author)

Notes / Sources

Chapter 1

1. Mackie, R. L. p. 94
2. Mackie, J. D. p. 43
3. ibid. p. 36
4. Scott p. 4
5. Mackie, J.D. p. 38
6. Mackie, R.L. p. 72
7. Tytler p. 4

Chapter 2

1. Traquair p. 11
2. Mackie, R.L. p. 97
3. ibid. p. 100
4. Barrow p. 21
5. Lanercost
6. Tytler p. 22

Chapter 3

1. Bryant pp. 147 – 157
2. Guisborough
3. Tytler p. 21
4. Bryant p. 169
5. Tytler p. 28
6. Scott p. 21

7. Mackie, J.D. p. 63
8. Barrow p. 52
9. Mackie, J.D. p. 39
10. Fordun
11. Barrow p. 72
12. Calendar of Documents Relating to Scotland
13. Mackie, R.L. p. 117
14. Turner
15. Tytler p. 46
16. ibid. p. 47
17. ibid. p. 48

Chapter 4

1. Scott p. 38
2. Tytler p. 54
3. Scott p. 50
4. Tytler p. 82
5. Traquair p. 124
6. Barrow p. 195
7. Scott p. 51
8. Barrow p. 204

Chapter 5

1. Traquair p. 128
2. Bower
3. ibid.
4. Barbour
5. Wyntoun
6. Scott p. 72
7. ibid., p. 73
8. Scalaronica
9. Barrow p. 210
10. Barbour
11. Barrow p. 213
12. Bingham p. 132

13. Traquair p. 141
14. Scalaronica
15. Palgrave
16. Calendar of Documents Relating to Scotland
17. Palgrave
18. ibid.
19. ibid.
20. Calendar of Documents Relating to Scotland
21. Fordun
22. Barbour

Chapter 6

1. Barbour
2. ibid.
3. Scott p. 102
4. Bingham p. 166
5. Traquair p. 150
6. Bingham p. 171
7. Scott p. 109
8. Barrow p. 257
9. McKisack p. 2
10. McNamee p. 49
11. Lanercost
12. ibid.
13. Scott p. 129
14. McKisack p. 30
15. Vita Edwardi Secundi
16. Barbour
17. Scott p. 145
18. Barrow p. 298
19. ibid. Chapter 12

Chapter 7

1. Lanercost
2. Barrow p. 333

3. McNamee p. 166
4. Lanercost
5. Bingham p. 260
6. Lanercost
7. Calendar of Documents Relating to Scotland
8. Lanercost
9. Scott p. 190
10. Barbour
11. Lanercost
12. McNamee p. 91
13. Scott p. 195
14. McKisack p. 65
15. ibid. p. 66

Chapter 8

1. Scott p. 201
2. Bingham p. 282
3. Lanercost
4. Scott p. 202
5. Barbour
6. Lanercost
7. Fordun
8. Tytler p. 144
9. Lanercost
10. McNamee p. 100
11. Le Bel (quoted in Scott, p. 218)
12. Traquair p. 229
13. The Close Rolls
14. ibid.
15. ibid.
16. ibid.
17. Barrow p. 345 (note 3)
18. Lanercost
19. ibid.
20. Gesta Edwardi; McNamee, p. 101

21. McNamee p. 101
22. Calendar of Documents Relating to Scotland
23. Lanercost
24. Scalaronica
25. Barrow p. 297
26. Scalaronica
27. Barbour
28. The Close Rolls
29. McNamee p. 100

Chapter 9

1. Barbour
2. Hayes
3. Graham
4. Gesta Edwardi
5. Barbour
6. ibid.
7. ibid.
8. ibid.
9. ibid.
10. Gesta Edwardi
11. Young p. 162
12. Barbour
13. Lanercost
14. McNamee p. 101
15. Barbour
16. Scalaronica
17. Lanercost
18. Fordun
19. Barbour
20. ibid.
21. Lanercost
22. The Close Rolls
23. Bingham p. 286
24. Barbour

Chapter 10

1. Barbour (Different figures for the amount of Richmond's ransom are given in some English chronicles. *Flores Historiarum,* Rolls Series, ed. Luard,iii, pp. 224-5, puts it at 14,000 marks, and the *Anonimalle Chronicle*, ed. Childs and Taylor, pp. 110-12, gives £3,000). Whatever the amount, it was so large it took a considerable time to raise despite King Edward's best efforts, with the Earl finally being released between May and September 1324.
2. Scott p. 204
3. Barbour
4. Tytler p. 145
5. Scott p. 204
6. Memorials of Beverley Minster
7. Lanercost
8. Gesta Edwardi
9. Nova Taxatio. Public Records Office.
10. Lanercost
11. ibid.
12. McKisack p. 75, Traquair p. 232
13. Lanercost
14. Vita Edwardi Secundi
15. Bingham p. 290
16. Tytler p. 146

Appendix A – The Treaty of Edinburgh/Northampton

1. McKisack p. 76 onwards
2. Tytler p. 148
3. Traquair p. 247
4. Stones, No. 41a
5. Barrow p. 366
6. ibid. p. 369
7. Barbour

Appendix B - Early 14th Century Armies

1. The Patent Rolls
2. The Close Rolls
3. Vita Edwardi
4. BL MS Stowe 553
5. Lanercost
6. Powicke

Great Seal of King Robert the Bruce. (Reproduction, author)

Select Bibliography

Primary

Anglo-Scottish Relations 1174 – 1328, ed. E. L. G. Stones, (Nelson, 1964)

Calendar of the Close Rolls (HMSO, London)

Calendar of the Patent Rolls (HMSO, London)

Calendar of Inquisitions Miscellaneous (HMSO, London)

Calendar of Documents Relating to Scotland, 5 vols. i-iv ed. J. Bain, (Edinburgh, 1881-4); v ed. G.G. Simpson & J.D. Galbraith (Scottish Record Office, 1988)

Chronicle of the Scottish Nation, John of Fordun, ed. W. F. Skene (Edinburgh 1872)

Documents and Records illustrating the History of Scotland, ed. F. Palgrave (Lyon Public Library 1837)

Gesta Edwardi de Carnarvan vol. ii of *Chronicles of the reigns of Edward I and Edward II,* ed. W. Stubbs (Rolls Series, 1883)

Memorials of Beverley Minster, ed. A. F. Leach (Surtees Society, 1903)

Orygynale Chronykil of Scotland, Andrew Wyntoun, ed. D. Laing (Edinburgh, 1872)

Nova Taxatio 1327, Public Records Office, E179

Scalacronica, by Sir Thomas Grey of Heton, Knight, ed. and trans. H. Maxwell (Glasgow, 1907)

Scotichronicon, Walter Bower, ed. D.E.R. Watt (Aberdeen, 1991)

The Bruce, John Barbour, ed. and translated A.A.M.Duncan (Edinburgh, 1997)

The Chronicle of Lanercost, ed. and translated H. Maxwell (Glasgow, 1913)

The Chronicle of Walter of Guisborough, ed. H. Rothwell, (Camden, 1957)

The True Chronicles of Jean le Bel, 1290 – 1360. Trans. N.Bryant, (Boydell & Brewer, 2011)

Vita Edwardi Secundi monachi cuiusdam Malmesberiensis: ed. N. Denholm-Young (London, 1957)
Wardrobe Book 1322 – 23 MS Stowe 553, British Library

Secondary

Barrow, G.W.S., *Robert Bruce, and the Community of the Realm of Scotland*, 3rd edition, (Edinburgh, 1988)
Bingham, Caroline, *Robert the Bruce*, (London, 1998)
Brown, Michael, *Bannockburn: The Scottish War and the British Isles, 1307-23,* (Edinburgh, 2008)
Bryant, Arthur, *A History of Britain and the British People, Volume 1, Set in a Silver Sea*, (London, 1984)
Butlin, Robin, (ed.), *Historical Atlas of North Yorkshire,* (Otley, 2003)
Graham, Lewis, *The Crosses of the North Yorkshire Moors,* (Whitby, 1993)
Haines, Roy Martin, *King Edward II: His Life, His Reign and its Aftermath, 1284-1330*, (Montreal, 2003)
Hayes, R. H., *Old Routes and Pannierways in North East Yorkshire,* (North York Moors National Park Authority, 1988)
Mackie, John Duncan, *A History of Scotland*, 2nd edition, (London, 1978)
Mackie, Robert L., *A Short History of Scotland*, (Oxford, 1931)
McKisack, May, *The Fourteenth Century,* The Oxford History of England, Vol. V. (Oxford, 1959)
McNamee, Colm, *The Wars of the Bruces,* (East Linton, 1997)
Phillips,Seymour, *Edward II,* (Yale, 2010)
Powicke, M., *Military Obligation in Medieval England* (Oxford, 1962)
Scott, Ronald McNair, *Robert the Bruce, King of Scots,* (London, 1982)
Spinks, Stephen, *Edward II, the Man, a Doomed Inheritance*, (Stroud, 2017)
Traquair, Peter, *Freedom's Sword, Scotland's War of Independence,* (London, 1998)
Turner, Hilary L., *Town Defences in England and Wales,* (London, 1970)
Tytler, Patrick Fraser, *History of Scotland,* Vol. I (Edinburgh,1864)
Warner, Kathryn, *Edward II, the Unconventional King,* (Stroud, 2015)
Young, Alan, and Stead, Michael, *In the Footsteps of Robert Bruce,* (Stroud, 1999)

14th C. wooden effigies in Church of St Martin, Allerton Mauleverer, one believed to be Sir John Mauleverer who fought at Bannockburn. (Author)

Acknowledgements

The author would like to acknowledge the contribution of the following individuals and organisations for their invaluable encouragement, inspiration, advice, guidance and assistance.

Chris Pye, Louise Whittaker, Chris Rock, Diane Lee, Miles Johnson, Janet Cochrane, Professor Anne Curry, Pete Jackson, Liz Kemp, Alex Ibbott, Colin Speakman, Keith Dowen, Simon Marsh, Chris May, Lucy Frontani, Penny Hayashi, Harriet Fielding, Geoffrey Carter, Ian Marr, Sandra Kennish, Richard Culmer, Mike Winterflood, Dean Davidson and the team at 3 Swords Historical Services, Michael Frost and the Masters of the Bench of the Inner Temple, the staff at the British Library reading room Boston Spa, Kaitlyn Krieg at the Morgan Museum, New York, and not forgetting all my friends and colleagues at the Sutton Bank National Park Centre.

I am especially grateful to the North York Moors National Park Authority for their generous support.

Thank you to the Battlefields Trust for their support of this endeavour over many years, and for use of the sketch maps of the battle.

Index

The Battle of Byland

14th of October

1322

The bronze plaque on the memorial stone commemorating 700 years since the battle. (Author)